ANGELS, INCENSE AND REVOLUTION:

CATHOLIC SCHOOLDAYS OF THE 1960s

Wanda Skowronska

Connor Court Publishing

Connor Court Publishing Pty Ltd

Copyright © Wanda Skowronska 2019

ALL RIGHTS RESERVED. This book contains material protected under International and Federal Copyright Laws and Treaties. Any unauthorised reprint or use of this material is prohibited. No part of this book may be reproduced or transmitted in any form or by any means, electronic or mechanical, including photocopying, recording, or by any information storage and retrieval system without express written permission from the publisher.

PO Box 7257
Redland Bay QLD 4165
sales@connorcourt.com
www.connorcourt.com

ISBN: 9781925501919

Cover design by Janusz Tydda. The front cover photo depicts Brigadine students sitting in the front garden of the school in 1966 and, below, a Corpus Christi procession within the grounds of Brigadine Convent in 1967 shown in the School Annual magazine of those years. (From the Brigadine Archives).

Printed in Australia

ANGELS, INCENSE AND REVOLUTION:

CATHOLIC SCHOOLDAYS OF THE 1960s

CONTENTS

Foreword	xi
Introduction	xiii
1. Was it a dream?	1
2. Reffos, jobs and the local Catholic school	15
3. School in Marrickville, Athens of the west	27
4. Baby boomers, stress and the Sacraments	37
5. Change and stability in the midst of sadness	57
6. Coogee, Mother Pascal and a new Dutch identity	63
7. Catholics and the world.	79
8. Silence, the Penny Catechism and attempts to gain wisdom	87
9. Unangelic behaviour and the plague	103
10. Choirs, gypsies and saints	107
11. Brigidine, baby boomers and crowded classes	117
12. Latin and the elixir of life	125
13. The singing nun and shunning the deceits the world	133
14. Truancy and swinish escapades	141
15. Friends from faraway places, my career as a smuggler	147
16. The lure of literature and language	153
17. Music, terror and Russian influences	165
18. Order and disorder in the cosmos	179
19. Rumours of revolution, the end of an era	187
20. Parting with an abiding rich heritage.	199
Endnotes	207

*Dedicated to
the wonderful and unforgettable
nuns, brothers and priests and all teachers
who transmitted to us the vision of things eternal*

Mass for the ordination of priests in 1963 in St Mary's Cathedral.

Nuns singing in one of the many processions at Brigidine Convent, Randwick, circa 1966. (Reprinted with permission).

ACKNOWLEDGEMENTS

This book could not have come about without the help of many who helped with stories, photos and information. In particular I would like to acknowledge the Sydney Archdiocesan archivist, Lienntje Cornelissen, for her help. I would also like to thank Brigidine nuns, Sr Marie Langtry, and Sr Kathleen Butler who gave me some materials pertaining to the Brigidine sisters; also thank you to the Good Samaritan archivist, Sr Lia van Haren, for her kind help. I also give heartfelt thanks to Francis Ridley, Peter Macinante, Marita Cudmore, Frank Borg, Gail Instance and Carmel Righetti whose photos were invaluable for this story which is not just about one person's schooldays but about an era as well. I would like to thank my friend Maureen O'Connor, who went through Brigidine, for encouraging me along the way and to all the friends, sisters, priests and friends who were part of 'those times' which seem so far away and yet so near.

Students at the procession commemorating Saint Maria Goretti at Saint Brigid's School, Marrickville. The young girl at the centre took on the role of the saint and children often closed their eyes when praying intensely.

Foreword

Enter any older Catholic church in Australia, from St Mary's Cathedral down to the not so humble average parish church. The hard shell, unchanged since construction, envelops the viewer with pillars and vaulting, stained glass and stations of the cross, for all the world as if the medieval Age of Faith were still with us. But what goes on inside is much altered from the time of Wanda Skowronska's evocative memoir, the 1960s. The Mass is still said and the faithful pray and organise charitable works, but the Catholic Church and schools are no longer in the business of providing the same complete and ordered vision of a life focussed on eternity as they once did. As Wanda remembers – with a vivid recall whose accuracy I as a contemporary can vouch for – a Catholic education created a total world of devotion which permeated all of life. "Culture" does not express the depth of penetration aimed at. The point of the "sensurround" of nuns, angelus, incense, hymns, sodalities, feast days, novenas, saints, first communions and confessions and the catechism was to create souls completely oriented to God and his commands. If some students let it wash over them or reacted against it, with many, like Wanda, the lesson took hold and flourished. Her soul, as recorded here, is a perfectly formed version of what the system aimed to produce. Her memoir is a perfect insight into the Australian Catholic past, as seen from the inside.

The second part of her story concerns the disappearance of that world, an event which occurred quite suddenly around 1969. The rebellious spirit of the times (as embodied, according to the nuns, in the *Johnny O'Keefe Show*) combined with the currents of change from the Second Vatican Council and the impact of *Humanae Vitae* to pull the rug from under the old order. As a child of refugees from Communist Eastern Europe, Wanda had a particular horror of socialist challenges to authority. Why would anyone throw over the splendid Catholic vision of the eternal for a mess of Communist-inspired agitprop and a few sub-pophymns.

A good question. Wanda's memoir will trigger in an older generation deep memories of what was lost and offer the younger generation an insight into an utterly different world.

James Franklin
Editor
Journal of the Australian Catholic Historical Society

Introduction

The following pages tell the story of what it was like for a 'reffo' kid to go to a Catholic school in Sydney around the time of the 1960s. It seems in hindsight I was standing on the edge of two eras, caught in some pivotal moments of that century's history, not knowing what it all meant, nor what was to come.

The nuns who taught us were hard-working, inspirational, with a defined sense of identity and their place in the world. They transmitted an entire worldview to us, with its inherited legacies and spiritual sensibilities.

Despite the looming deconstruction of much of the Western world, the rising anti-Christian culture wars, despite Sartre, Foucault and Derrida, the nuns that I encountered made safe havens for children who came their way, whether rich or poor, from settled or from broken families, or from many ethnic backgrounds. They created a unique world of eternal horizons and the following pages describe some of its realities – hopefully entertaining as well as serious – remembered with gratitude and love. It looks back mainly from a child's perspective of 'being there', with simple, youthful and unsophisticated perceptions occasionally intermingled with reflections in hindsight.

What follows are just filaments of its realities, of a time that once was, impressions of incense, angels and light through stained glass windows, as if from some Antipodean Cistercian monastery I once lived in, with its enduring poignant memories.

1
Was it a Dream?

For most of my life, never, ever, did I have any intention of writing about my schooldays. Until, that is, I noticed as I was getting older, that any reference to them made me seem like an alien who had just arrived from another galaxy. It dawned on me that I was not an alien but that the Catholic school world I had been part of had been so utterly a different world from the one we now inhabit, to the point of seeming an ethereal, distant dream. I had no idea that the 1960s and the Catholic schools in which I moved, walked and talked – whose teachers were mostly nuns – constituted the last vestiges of a twilight that was about to disappear. And yet, its transcendent vision did not disappear. For some of us at least it would forever echo in our memories in a profound way, strangely present and distant at the same time.

My formative years of schooling started just at the end of the 1950s and continued throughout the 1960s, to be precise from 1958 until 1969. They occurred before, during, and after the historic and turbulent years of Vatican II (1962-1965) though during most of this time, I had no idea, and indeed many students had no idea, that such a council was proceeding, let alone what a Vatican Council was, nor what it would portend. In my Antipodean milieu, full of sunshine, Irish hymns and hope, we lived and moved in a different world, with its age-old Catholic worldview still being transmitted as a daily routine, a vision and a reasoned account of the world. We saw nuns around us, prayed before and after classes, went to Mass, sang hymns in Latin, wore medals of Our Lady and saints around our necks, saw statues in every church and assumed angels surrounded us in classrooms and on the street. Many of us paid visits to the Blessed Sacrament in churches near our schools as a matter of course and called on St Jude, hope of the hopeless, to help us on many occasions.

Like Wordsworth in his 'Ode to Immortality', we might say that what we had seen seems 'apparelled in celestial light' and it has the 'glory and freshness of a dream' and might add: 'It is not now as it hath been of yore ... The things which I have seen I now can see no more'. But – and this is a big but – I am not just nostalgically sipping wine, reminiscing about the 'good old days'. I refer to the disappearance of a world. In the past half century we have witnessed the transformation of Western civilisation which still held sway in my youth, with its prevailing (though yes, declining) Judeo-Christian beliefs. Within a decade of my leaving school, the secular liberal expansion and anti-Catholic animus had clearly grown. The young were encouraged to forget the past, particularly their Judeo-Christian heritage, to an extent that overturned the world I had known. Many came to echo the anti-authoritarianism and cultural confrontations of the Frankfurt school and the French barricades, without being even aware of it. I was left, along with others, gazing down a long, long corridor past doors and windows onto charred fields beyond. Many of us who were educated just before and during the 1960s, who had known a different world, were left wondering what had happened, with haunting memories of an era's spiritual landscape. My school years were precisely on a pivot point – between one world and another.

My intention in this brief memoir is not to rail against current schools, nor to claim my experience as typical – for each person's memories of school are unique and good schools and teachers can be found in every age – but to reflect on and express gratitude for the Catholic education I had. There was something truly extraordinary about it and the 'ordinary' days of half a century ago. The nuns who taught me communicated a vision threaded with spiritual and philosophical meaning, particularly in the primary school years, in giving us competence in basic skills but, above all, transmitting a Catholic worldview pointing to infinite horizons. They transmitted an entire culture! From this type of education arose a definite sense of a mission which we all seemed to take for granted: that our teachers would educate, immerse and draw young people into the things of eternity and this would permeate all our days, and we would transmit it too. It really did happen; it was not a dream. I remember – I was there! No-one can deny me my memories!

I know, however, that many have had different experiences in their Catholic schools, some better, some worse, some much, much worse, and I pay respect to the fact that there were some who caused suffering to young people. But my own experience was different. Looking back from the new millennium, I feel, as time passes, that I am looking at a lost Atlantis that opened a door to the spiritual riches of the past 2,000 years and more. It meant a lot to a poor child of refugees like me; and beyond my particular experience, I am looking in more general terms at how a culture gets transmitted, as it *was* transmitted to me during the late fifties and early sixties. Perhaps some details will resonate with those who are reading this.

Please do not get me wrong, this is not any final word on education, nor on the history of Catholic education, just some *reflections* on a time that has gone, as I give witness to the fact that it happened ...

Australia, Antarctica and St Brigid

My Catholic schooling was in Australia, that outpost of colonial life which is one of the last stops before Antarctica. The Sydney schools I attended were 'typical' Catholic schools in one way, as many would remember, in that they were squat brick buildings near a church and had mostly nuns as teaching staff. Nuns were like the planets of the solar system – they were just there. They were such a consistent presence in most Catholic schools and hospitals when I was growing up that, as Mark Massa says, during the 1950s and 1960s they were the most likely 'icon' of things Catholic in the eyes of millions of children, hospital patients and the disabled.[1] They did not suddenly appear but represented the strong tradition of transmitting the Catholic faith to the four corners of the globe, a strong commitment that had been going on for centuries despite persecutions and wars. In the 1960s nuns were looked up to, if not exactly as one might regard the Pope, then nearly so, as if they were his close friends and confidantes, who knew his plans, what they were doing, and what the Church was doing.

While the schools I attended were typical in many ways, my experiences were somewhat atypical in that I was not of Anglo-Celtic background, as were most students in Catholic schools during the 1950s and 60s. I was a reffo kid, a child of post-World War II Polish and Latvian refugees who were at the mercy of that War's unpredictable historical, economic and psychological consequences. Like other migrants, we moved a few times, seeking jobs, were often confused, adapting to changed family circumstances as best we could. On further consideration, perhaps my experience in Catholic schools was typical – precisely in being part of those post-World War II population shifts from Europe to America, Australia and other Western countries and having within it the socio-cultural dynamic of those times. This was the era of Bob Menzies, street newspaper sellers, factories, New Australians, fruit shops, milk bars, double-decker buses, coconut ice and great Catholic processions. And in those heady times, Catholic schools were a stabilising influence in changing family circumstances and a changing world. They certainly were for me. There was no hint of neutrality or secularism in such schools, and on entering their world, you quickly learned to relate to God, the Virgin Mary, the angels and the ever-present Communion of Saints. St Michael the Archangel definitely had a sword and huge wings – we never doubted it! Catholic schools were a world unto themselves.

My primary education was at two Catholic schools, both called St Brigid's, one in the seaside Sydney suburb of Coogee and the other in Marrickville, an area of inner-west Sydney which was a place for many migrants to obtain cheaper housing in the 1960s.

Sydney was inundated with parish schools named after saints whose history went back centuries. Many were named after St Brigid (the fifth century Irish saint, not the 14th century Swedish one of the same name) or a multitude of other Irish saints as most Catholics in the early colony were Irish. Thus schools were not only named after the eternally present realities of Catholic life – Christ the King, Our Lady of Lourdes, Saint Joseph, Our Lady of the Annunciation, The Holy Innocents – but also especially named after the Irish saints – St Declan, St Finbar, St Kevin, St Aidan, St Columbus, St Finian, St Patrick and so on. This was a fact which any migrant, whether Italian, Polish, Portuguese, Hungarian or Chinese, was soon confronted with: the reality that the Catholic world within Australia at that time was largely Irish and threaded with stories of Irish missionaries. There were high concentrations of Catholics of Irish descent in inner city suburbs. But one Irish farming town south of Sydney, as Edmund Campion relates, had so many Irish families in it that it was known as the Tipperary of Australia so if you threw a stone down a street in Boorowa, it would surely hit a Ryan, a Dwyer, a Hurley or a Corcoran.[2] If asked whether one had been to Ireland, one might hear the response, 'No, but I've been to Booroowa'! In other words, at some point, it was inevitable that we would acquire an Irish dimension to our personalities, So those Portuguese, Chinese or Hungarian immigrants came to know 'When Irish Eyes are Smiling' and 'Danny Boy' within a few years and I could say, at age eight, the words 'Saint Columbkille' with greater ease than I could utter the words 'meat pie and chips please'.

Nuns set out for Australia: Nietzsche was wrong – God remained alive

When the religious nuns set out for Australia in the nineteenth century, they were on a remarkable journey, historically and spiritually. As the history of the parish schools in this country, as in most colonial countries, inevitably rests on the arrival of religious nuns there, it is apt to make a brief comment on them.

In Australia, the earliest nuns in the Colony were Sisters of Charity. These Irish nuns set out from Cork in Ireland and arrived in Sydney in 1838 at the request of Benedictine Bishop John Bede Polding (1794-1877), to take care of the poor and marginalised in Sydney, and this they did with great commitment. Bishop Polding, who was to become Australia's first archbishop, himself had a noted positive rapport with the convicts sent here, giving retreats to many thousands of them.[3] Not long after his arrival, in fulfilment of the bishop's dream, the first Australian religious order was established in 1857, the Good Samaritan Sisters, which was to continue and expand charitable work in the spirit of Saint Benedict. In Benedictine fervour, Bishop Polding tried to insert a stronger English mould into Australian Catholicism but by most accounts had very limited success as Irish influences were generally too powerful – even if ultimately a unique Anglo-Celtic mix came to be.

Most of my education came from an Irish order which sailed the high seas from Ireland to Australia. They were named the Sisters of St Brigid and this order was established in 1807 by Bishop Daniel Delaney in Tullow in Ireland, in honour of the great fifth century saint of Kildare. But they became familiarly known as 'the Brigidines'. A year later, the same bishop also founded a community of men and named them the Brothers of St Patrick or the

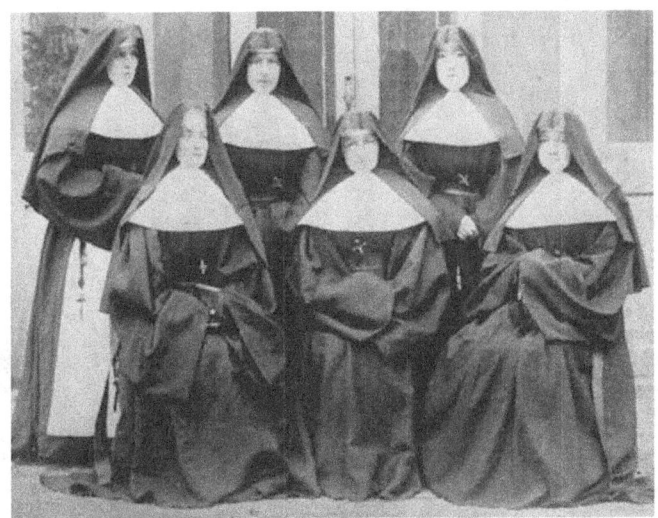

The pioneering Brigidine nuns who sailed to from Ireland on the ship *Chimborazo* in 1883 to set up schools in Australia. The oldest Catholic school in Australia, Parramatta Marist High, had been founded in 1820 by Fr John Therry while St Mary MacKillop's first school for poor Catholic children was set up in 1866. The first Brigidine school opened in Coonamble soon after the sisters arrived in 1883.

The original Brigidine convent in Ireland in Tullow where Fr Daniel Delaney formed the Brigidines. He insisted that he was not founding a new congregation but rather re-founding the Order of St. Brigid of Kildare which had existed in Ireland from the fifth to the sixteenth century until the monasteries were suppressed in that century. From this re-formation of the convent, the nuns were to spread out to all parts of the world.

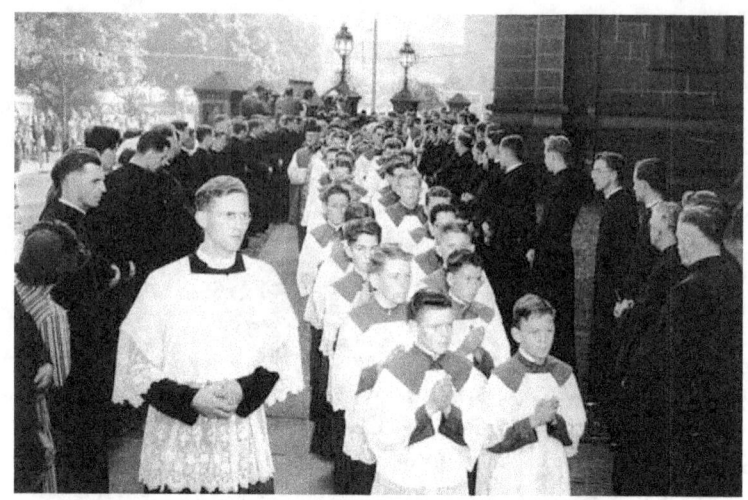

This was emblematic of the Catholic world I entered. Here is a procession of altar boys during the Eucharistic Congress of 1953 which happened not long before I enrolled at St Brigid's Catholic school in 1958.
(From the Archives of the Catholic Archdiocese of Sydney).

St Mary's Cathedral the opening of the Eucharistic Congress in 1953.
(From the Archives of the Catholic Archdiocese of Sydney).

A rare large group photo of nuns attending the Eucharistic Congress of 1953. The Carmelites and other contemplative sisters remained in their enclosed orders. (From the Archives of the Catholic Archdiocese of Sydney).

Part of the long procession of priests during the 1953 Eucharistic Congress. (From the Archives of the Catholic Archdiocese of Sydney).

One of the many outdoor processions of the 1953 Eucharistic Congress. The Blessed Sacrament was carried throughout the streets of Sydney. Members of other religious faiths came to watch.
(From the Archives of the Catholic Archdiocese of Sydney).

Legion of Mary members at the time of the Eucharistic Congress 1953. This was one of the many flourishing groups in the church at that time.
(From the Archives of the Catholic Archdiocese of Sydney).

Was it a dream?

Patricians. These were not easy times for the Irish. Bishop Daniel Delaney had grown up under severe penal laws in Ireland and cared greatly for the fate of his people. His father had died in youth and when he decided to become a priest in 1763, at the age of sixteen, with the help of a good Protestant friend he was smuggled out of the country to a college in Paris to begin his studies for the priesthood. In 1770, Daniel Delany was ordained a priest – significantly the year that Captain Cook entered Botany Bay. On his return to Ireland, disguised as a layman, he was shocked at the poverty and social breakdown there. However, he was determined to help his people and was inspirational in restoring education (a proud tradition of the Irish that had been abolished under the Penal Laws), and the Brigidines grew and grew. They were soon to touch the lives of many in Australia, including mine.

On 6 January 1883, a group of Brigidine sisters at Mountrath, south of Dublin, heard a priest, Fr Andrew Phelan, tell of 'a distant colony' called Australia, the land under the Southern Cross, pervaded by heat, droughts and dust storms and with dioceses larger than all Ireland![4] It may as well have been China or Mongolia. At the request of Bishop Murray of Maitland, Fr Phelan asked for volunteers to undertake the education of the poor children there who in many places had no-one to educate them. The nuns and priests were aware of the Irish 'potato orphans', who had either fled Ireland's potato famine or been forcibly moved to all corners of the world including Australia. Because of the *Public Instruction Act of 1880*, which aimed at developing a comprehensive school system in the Colony of New South Wales (as in the other Australian Colonies), many children were faced with a secular education or none at all, and this did not bode well for the vitally important transmission of the Catholic faith which mattered immensely – in fact was a matter of life and death – to subsequent generations including myself, one of the 'poor' children who would receive the cultural wealth deriving from this view.

Interestingly, shortly before this, Mary MacKillop (Saint Mary of the Cross, Australia's first saint), with help from her brother, John MacKillop, had set up a schoolroom in Penola in 1866 to teach 40 students. It was here that the Sisters of St Joseph of the Sacred Heart began their mission, similar to that of the Brigidines and other orders in other places. Transmission of a true Catholic culture was the issue of the day, a remarkable co-operative effort for those who were poor or not, indigenous, Anglo-Celtic or refugees, anyone from anywhere.

Back in Ireland, six brave Brigidine Sisters were chosen out of the sixteen who had volunteered to go to faraway Australia. They sailed on the SS *Chimborazo* in 1883 and the Irish *Freeman's Journal* commented on their departure: 'To carry out this great mission of the Irish Church, the Sisters of Mountrath have left a happy home and the country they dearly loved. They go with the benediction of the present Holy Father ...'[5] The musical talents of the sisters enabled them to lead the ship's passengers in singing during the trip as many were so depressed, as were the nuns themselves, thinking they might never see Ireland again. They sailed via Naples, Port Said, Melbourne and Sydney to reach their final destination, Coonamble, where, with great difficulties they set up their first school in New South Wales, with some rooms for living and most for teaching. Soon other Catholic communities asked the Brigidine sisters to establish schools for them. In 1887 five sisters went to Cooma; seven to Cowra in 1894; and in 1898 another six to New Zealand.

From the outset, wherever they were, the nuns and the students faced many practical obstacles, not least being that of disease (typhoid, scarletina and measles took the lives of nuns and students) in an era before immunisation could help. They received no salary and only survived on the donations of parents who could pay the modest fees. From this grew many schools run by the Brigidines

Was it a dream?

in several Australian states (as also grew schools run by orders like the Josephites, Mercy nuns, Good Samaritans and other orders) and it was into this great pioneering heritage of Catholic schools I was inducted about 70 years after their first arrival, as a reffo kid of Polish-Latvian background, yet to learn where Ireland was, and what it was. Despite illness and death, the Great Transmission continued, no matter what.

While Nietzsche may have claimed 'God is dead' in the previous century, God was in fact very much alive in every urban parish in the 1950s and 60s, in the priests and nuns I saw as a young child in the schools I attended. Parents and children lined up to see the nuns, churches overflowed on Sundays, and the missionary spirit of St Columbanus, St Declan and St Patrick crisscrossed Australia.

There had been a grand Eucharistic procession on the streets of Sydney just a few years before (in 1953) I enrolled in school in 1958. *The Sydney Morning Herald* reported that in this procession were New South Wales mounted police, acolytes, altar-boys, the Australian flag, and the Papal flag escorted by two Papal Knights.[6] Then came the Blessed Sacrament banner, followed by altar boys from St. Peter's, Surry Hills, schoolgirls, national groups wearing traditional costumes, then members of the Caledonian Catholic Association, the Irish National Association. the Children of Mary (6,000 lined the streets, over 350 were in the procession) in their blue capes and white dresses, then two girls representing each (!) parish in Sydney, students, representatives of the Third Order of Our Lady of Mt. Carmel, Theresians, Catholic nurses, men from Catholic friendly societies and the Holy Name Society, St. Vincent de Paul Society and University graduates and undergraduates. Next came nuns, brothers, seminarians (352 of them!) and regular clergy wearing the habits of their orders, followed by clergy in choir dress and Sydney diocesan clergy in albs and chasubles. Finally came Cardinal Gilroy and the Papal Legate, who carried the Monstrance (written with capital 'M' in the *Sydney Morning Herald*). In the evening, the same paper reports an evening gathering at the Showground which elicited roars of welcome for the Cardinal and his guests:

> The Papal Legate, Cardinal Gilroy, the Patriarch of the Armenians, Cardinal Agagianian, and the Archbishop of Bombay, Cardinal Gracias, were greeted with a roar as they entered the section of the Members' Stand allocated to the clergy.[7]

This was the world I entered as a post-war reffo kindergarten kid: that wide, diverse, rich universe which then surrounded Australian Catholics. Moreover, without ever considering themselves feminists or philosophers, the nuns of that era seemed, very simply, to have proven Nietzsche wrong. God, and the Church Nearly-Triumphant here in Australia, in every suburb, was very much in evidence. The sisters had a clear sense of identity and translated this into everyday life in their role as teachers.

2

Reffos, Jobs and the Local Catholic School

One summer's day there we were, kindergarten children standing near the doorway of St Brigid's school, Coogee, on our very first day in our black box-pleat tunic over a white shirt (many Australian school children wore this whether in public or Catholic schools). How did it happen that I was there in very European plaits and ribbons in my hair, looking every inch a 'new Australian'? It was the same way as for other Catholics whose parents enrolled their children in the Catholic parish school closest to where they were living at the time. In those years, you could be confident, in urban centres, that there was a Catholic school near you. In 1958 we were living with relations in Randwick. My mother's sister and husband, Zenia and Lazar Kulic, like my parents, had come to Australia as post-war refugees, called DPs (Displaced Persons). In the aftermath of World War II, Ben Chifley, Prime Minister of Australia (1945-1949) established the Federal Department of Immigration which was to bring in refugees and migrants to help defend Australia. After a stay in Bathurst Migrant Camp, Zenia and Lazar had moved to Sydney, managing to put a deposit on an old house in Randwick, after Zenia had plied her dentistry skills in the camp and been paid for some of it. The reason they bought in Randwick was that it was relatively close to the glass factory where uncle Lazar worked. He had a degree in agriculture but it was unrecognised in Australia – as many such degrees were then – so, like many immigrants with university degrees, he worked in a factory. Though the house they bought was old, it was an amazing purchase for a refugee, but at that time things were cheaper in Sydney. So we all somehow pitched in and fitted in. Zenia and Lazar lived in one room; my parents, Bogdan and Valerie, lived in another room; the children, Michael and myself in another; and when my paternal grandmother, Maria Wanda Skowronska, arrived she slept on a bed in the kitchen. There was nothing unusual in this – many migrant families know this type of accommodation story only too well, some temporarily, some permanently, of using every nook and cranny for sleeping purposes for a while, of gathering around the table, trying to make sense of work, life and survival in 'Aauustraaalija'.

In this reffo world, while trying to crawl out of penury, many carried wounds from another world. During World War II, my mother had been severely wounded by metal shrapnel ripping open her back, in a bomb explosion in Germany; my father had been shot several times in the Warsaw Uprising and carried bullets to his German prison; my grandmother had been in a concentration camp for four years (Ravensbrück); my uncle Lazar fled those who wanted to kill him in Yugoslavia; my aunt Zenia also survived several bombings; my grandfather in Latvia had been murdered by the Communists – which covers just a few people in my family. The family home had been bombed in east Latvia and I had relations in gulags. However, these post-war refugees were fairly cheerful given all this – they were young and trying to make a new life, to live, to love, to survive. This was the era where there was no Trauma Counselling, no migrant outreach groups or, if there were, hardly anyone knew about them. These young adults, like so many Jewish and other post-war survivors of horrors beyond description, just went to work each day and did their best in 'Aauustraaalija', which gave them some peace, though not always forgetfulness, and a chance for a future. And many of their children went to Catholic schools run by very energetic, Irish Australian nuns.

Reffos, jobs and the local Catholic school

I knew nothing of the world, having spent my earliest five years in Bonegilla, a 'Migrant and Reception' Centre for post World War II refugees who lived in simple army barrack huts. It was Eden for me which Sydney could not easily replace. But I well remember my aunt and uncle's old house in Randwick, whose wooden planks were so old one could sometimes see the soil beneath. It had an exciting feature I had never seen before, a mysterious structure called a Hills Hoist, in the back yard which offered imaginary hijinks to children. My cousin Michael and I tried to reach up to hang on it, so we could swirl around on this clothes line. From that part of Randwick it was not far to walk to the 'sand dunes' of South Coogee, an unknown land where camels might appear, where one could be an explorer in the desert. It was the era of Holdens, trams, Vincent's and Bex powders, exciting Milo, Surf, Persil and Omo (which was whiter than white of course), peanut butter sandwiches, corner shops and lollies in jars. I got to do shopping errands for Auntie Zenie at Mr Greenhorn's corner shop in Rainbow St, Randwick, and gazed longingly at tall jars of lollies. I was sometimes sent to buy a Vincent's powder – by the single wrapped unit – for my aunt, a relatively cheap way to assuage headaches, trauma and loss. The adults tried to create fun for the children, visiting parks, seeing Australian gum trees, and marvelling at the local birds. In one family expedition, we saw the snake man of La Perouse and were all astonished at this apogé of human experience.

Each day, however, was mostly a long, hard grind. Many migrants worked to save a deposit for a house or, if possible, start a business. Some saved especially to buy a Holden after they got their first jobs, as that was an enormous status symbol. None of us had a Holden. Apart, that is, from my mother's cousin Veronica who with her husband Juzef, two children, Lucy and Anna, and her parents, happened to live on the 'outskirts of Sydney', that is, in Pagewood, a few kilometres away. They had come out as DPs too, and been sent first to Silver City Migrant Camp, north of Sydney, and then on to Dalby in Queensland (the family had been sent all over to different migrant camps). They worked and paid back their passage to Australia and then returned to Sydney to be with the rest of us. Like the Italians, Maltese and Portuguese, they sought work in factories in this area – it was then certainly much cheaper to live in than now. To the admiration of all, auntie Veronica purchased a Holden, with a discount, as she and Juzef had a Polish friend who worked in the Pagewood Holden factory and a typical photo was taken of a 'migrant made good' standing in front of a lime-green Holden. But, it could not be sent to relations in Stalinist Latvia, as the police would have arrested anyone who received such a shocking capitalist symbol. So we simply admired Uncle Juzef's 'standing near the Holden' photo here in Australia.

Holden or no Holden, the pressing migrant task was education for the children. This would assuage all the problems of life. It would give a secure future in an era where local schools were utterly trusted as institutions of learning. And coming from countries with distinctly Catholic heritages, my parents enrolled me in Kindergarten in St Brigid's, Coogee, a squat brick building with a grand Romanesque church next to it, with palm trees and flowers surrounding it all. This was a continuation of their heritage. There was a large 'mission' house next to it which I only learned later was where Missionaries of the Sacred Heart stayed before heading off as intrepid adventurers and missionaries to the South Seas, with a thousand stories of bravery to be told.

I just sat in class, not being able to speak English, as was the case with many migrant children. I had spoken every language but English in Bonegilla, being able to say 'hello' in Hungarian and Estonian to DPs there, but not in English. My cousin Michael

A group of Brigidine nuns at a gathering in Echuca (Victoria) around mid C20. In 1886 a second Brigidine foundation was established in Echuca at the request of Bishop Crane of Sandhurst.

Another religious group very visible on the streets of Sydney mid last century: Our Lady's Nurses for the Poor or, 'The Brown Nurses', who often visited the poor in their homes. The group called Our Lady's Nurses for the Poor was founded in Sydney in 1913 by a young Australian woman Eileen O'Connor and a priest from the Missionaries of the Sacred Heart, Father Edward McGrath.

Nuns from the Sisters of St Joseph of the Sacred Heart (the Josephites) founded by St Mary McKillop who opened the first Catholic school in 1866 in Penola, South Australia. The rule for the order was written by Fr Tennison Woods in 1867. Here are Josephite nuns all from the same family, circa 1955.

The St Brigid's School Parish Hall in Coogee, Sydney, with the school to the right, where the Brigidine nuns taught. In the hall, grand Kindergarten Balls were held and Irish dancing, singing and athletic prowess was taught. A local lady, Mrs King, came here voluntarily to play piano renditions of 'Pride of Erin' and 'Alley Cat'.

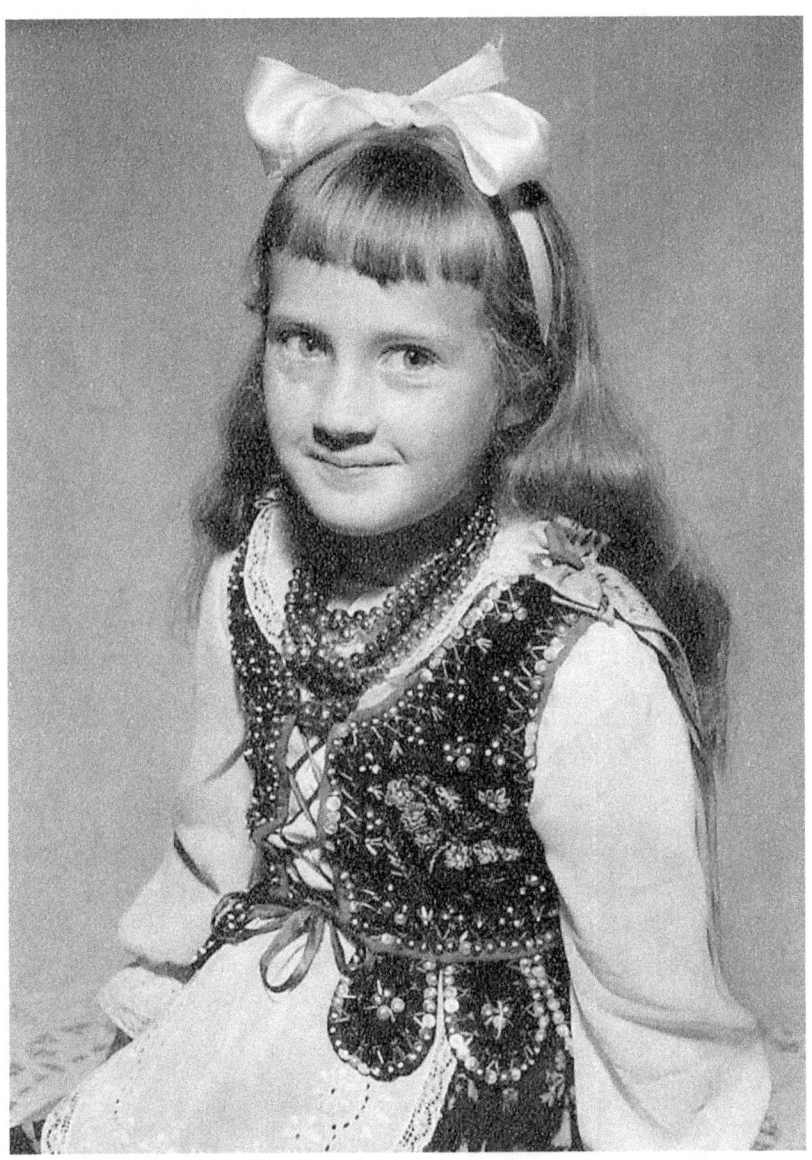

Here am I wearing the Polish national costume called 'Krakowianka', not daring to open my mouth as I was missing a few front teeth. This was the national costume in which at age 5, though utterly terrified, I was awarded first prize at the Kindergarten Ball in 1958.

Here is Frank Borg at right with his playmate, in typical cowboy gear from the 1950s-60s era. There were countless battles fought in the backyards of Sydney between cowboys and the rest of the world with 'dead bodies' strewn over parks and backyards.

This was the era of processions for many different feast days. This photo shows a typical group of that era dating from 1954 in Augathella in Queensland.

was a 'big boy', knew English well and was already in first class, in an infants' co-ed class. I remember watching the weird goings on in class as an 'outsider' but I quickly learned the words 'lolly' and 'cream bun', as these were colourful features of the simple school tuck shop, and soon knew the name of nearly all the foods in Australia! (I still believe that learning names of food and drink is a great way 'into' a new language!). Michael, a year older, informed me of many things such as how to tell the time, how to climb fences and play chasings. I recall the kindergarten classroom and playing with blocks. I also recall the ignominious day that my cousin and I feigned illness, holding our stomachs pitifully yelling and crying, as we wanted to go home. My aunt was called to take us away. I don't know how a five and six year got away with it but we did. After infant school, as was the custom, my cousin went to De La Salle Boys' school nearby so we could not try the stunt of feigning sickness together again.

Roy Rogers, Annie Oakley, Davy Crockett and the Kindergarten Ball

The event that really stands out in my memory in 1958 was the St Brigid's Kindergarten Fancy Dress Ball. This was High Society in an era when every Australian child wanted to dress up as plastic- gun-toting Roy Rogers, Davy Crockett, Hopalong Cassidy, Annie Oakley or a Hawaiian hula-hula dancer in a grass skirt. All around Australia, from Cootamundra to Bundaberg, from Darwin to Devonport, in every capital city, children especially dressed as cowboys and multitudes of girls 'shot' their brothers, cousins and friends, dressed as Annie Oakley or as 'Injuns' with bows and arrows. Bodies were strewn everywhere. My friend Terry Lavis told me of her vivid memories when she was often an 'Injun' fighting her cowboy brothers in the yard around their house in Bathurst with her homemade bow and arrow. She was a skilled 'Injun' and offered the cowboys strong resistance. My cousin Michael, his neighbourhood friends Barry and Russell and I, often ran around shooting each with water pistols, in post-war, peacetime Australia.

Babcia arrives

It was at this time that my grandmother, who had survived the concentration camp, came out from Poland. Permission was hardly ever given to leave a Communist country. As survivor of a concentration camp, however, an exception was made for a two-year visit to Australia by Babcia (which all Polish grandmothers are called). My father was overwhelmed with emotion seeing his mother for the first time in nearly 20 years, in fact, we all were. He had not seen her since he was a child, for she was arrested early in the war, doing some espionage in a Polish underground organisation, the White Eagle. She was a great Polish patriot and, along with her sister and niece, had been arrested in Lublin, tortured, and then taken to Ravensbrück where she endured unspeakable horrors. To add to the sadness, her husband had disappeared. But ever optimistic, she found her daughter in an orphanage in post-war Poland and then sailed over the seas with her in loving anticipation of meeting her son and the family with presents for all. I received a typical Polish national costume, a 'Krakowianka', which was given to me with great flourish. A decision was made that I must wear it to the St Brigid's Kindergarten Ball. There was no alternative – my grandmother, my Babcia, must not have carried this traditional costume from Communist Poland in vain. Poland had survived the Nazis, and would survive the Communists. Poland would rise again independent, and Wanda's national costume would be evidence of it! In fact it fitted perfectly. So there I stood in a multi-coloured skirt, sparkling beads, frilly apron, ribbons and little black shoes, the emblem of Poland. My hair was plaited and tied with red ribbons – no Hawaiian hula-hula skirt or Annie Oakley garb for me!

Reffos, jobs and the local Catholic school

As things turned out, a 'Krakowianka' costume had never been seen in the entire history of St Brigid's in Coogee. It was a sensation! The school was located in a still very Anglo-Irish area, in fact one of the heartlands of Irish Catholic Australia. There were many raised eyes as I walked into the hall. The parents and 'judges' were so taken by it, that my attire was awarded first prize. My father in a suit, mother in a nice dress, and Babcia in a faux fur jacket, were so proud. But I was terrified when my name was called out to collect the prize thinking I was about to receive some punishment, not knowing what it was all about. A teacher kindly took my hand and led me to the stage. In my multi-coloured finery, the representative of Poland and all eastern Europe, standing mournfully next to the judges, waiting for some guillotine to drop, I was presented with a package that happily turned out to be a box of Roses chocolates which cheered me up instantly. I lost no time in opening it on stage and putting one in my mouth. At this I was promptly hauled off for this unexpected and unseemly behaviour.

In later years I shared stories of such fancy dress balls with my friend Gail Instance who told me she was once dressed as Fu Manchu for her Catholic primary school fancy dress ball in Queensland. She did not want to be Fu Man Chu but was nevertheless dressed as him as a costume was available. She was a most despondent Fu Man Chu and recalled how she walked along a Brisbane street to get to her local ball, in her chinoiserie, to the amazement of her neighbours. No doubt, she too was a sensation among the Hawaiian hula-skirts and cowboys which dominated the day. She has never forgotten being Fu Man Chu in Brisbane, as I have never forgotten being a Polish 'Krakowianka' at St Brigid's in Coogee.

This was the usual box pleat uniform and little suitcase carried by typical schoolchildren – whether at state or Catholic schools – in the 1950s and 1960s. Here is my friend Robyn Tandy on her very first day of school at Our Lady of Dolours, Chatswood, in Sydney.

3

SCHOOL IN MARRICKVILLE, ATHENS OF THE WEST

Things were soon to change. My parents did not stay in Randwick long. After a year, they ended up moving to Holmesdale Street, Marrickville, and our lives changed all over again. Most migrants wanted to buy a little place, no matter how small, to call their own. Our few belongings were piled into a hired van as we drove off to a new adventure. My parents had put a deposit on a small semi-detached house – a 'semi' – next to another owned by a nice Chinese couple. In Holmesdale Street, there lived a motley group of migrants and Aussies. Multiculturalism simply existed – there was no philosophy behind it. People just got on together in this land of peace called Australia, strange as it was with its drawling idiomatic expressions and daily linguistic adventures and misunderstandings. This cheap inner city suburb was far from fashionable then but at least in this way I got to see and experience some of the authentic, marginalised life of the inner city suburbs.

As my parents had to work very long hours, it fell to my grandmother Babcia Wanda to enrol me at the nearby Catholic school. By a weird turn of events, Babcia Wanda had ended up staying in Australia and had not returned to Soviet Poland as she was supposed to, after a certain time. She became very ill during her stay here and was supposed to die of stomach cancer. Thus she was unexpectedly granted permanent residence here by the Australian government. I remember I was taken to see her to say 'goodbye', and the atmosphere of the hospital room where she lay was overwhelmingly sad. I was lifted to kiss her for the last time as she lay so pale beneath white sheets. But Babcia did not die. She lived another 30 years! Whether the cure was miraculous or surgical I don't know but many people prayed for her. She, who had survived a concentration camp, had now survived terminal cancer! So she stayed and her newly obtained permanent residence in Australia was a boon to us all.

One day, in January 1959, Babcia took me to do the formalities for being enrolled in a school which also happened to be called St Brigid's in Marrickville. You would think this easy, but no. Babcia spoke little English and somehow she insisted to the enrolling staff that I had completed first class (taking this for kindergarten) and so I was mistakenly placed in second class. After all, that's how they do it in Poland! I am sure many migrants have similar stories. To give her due credit, Babcia had tried to learn English on the ship coming out to Australia. But as the classes had expressions like, 'Would you like a Devonshire tea and scones with a dollop of strawberry jam?' in the first lessons, she gave up. She would have uttered something like 'Matka Boska' ('O Mother of God') under her breath. English as a Second Language (ESL) programs were not as well developed then as they are nowadays. She actually called English 'the devil's language' and never studied it again.

Marrickville was a variegated, interesting suburb with many wooden and brick houses and semis, several factories, children with thin legs running barefoot on the streets, exotic shops on Marrickville Road and beautiful old churches. It seemed full of immigrants then, especially Greeks and Italians who set up shops – memorable milk bars and delicatessens. Never were there so many reminders of glories of ancient Greece – the Acropolis, Parthenon and Olympia – as there were on the streets of Sydney at that time. I recall walking with Babcia past the Greek shops along Marrickville

Road every day on the way to school with various enticing things on display. Rarely could we enjoy the illustrious gastronomic luxury of such places, but we gazed at and admired them. A current memoir of this era says:

> The main shopping strip of Marrickville Road was dominated by Greek shopkeepers. Taking up business was not always without problems for the new migrants. Giannis (Jack) Cordatos, one of Marrickville's most prominent Greek migrants, had to resort to subterfuge to purchase the Classic Milk Bar. The owners did not want to sell to southern Europeans but were impressed by French speakers. Cordatos changed his name to Revel and won the sale. Marrickville became known throughout Sydney as 'the Athens of the west'.[8]

While Marrickville may have been called the 'Athens of the west', there were few Poles or Latvians in the area, as they tended to live mainly in Ashfield, Bankstown and further out west. But here we were amidst the Greek glories. On top of this, I continued my Irish inculturation at the new school. However, as well as the traditional Irish hymns we sang at Saint Brigid's, I began to hear and remember Polish and Latvian Catholic hymns – a growing exposure to the universality of the Church. This was because my mother and I went to the Latvian Catholic community's Mass at Saint Dominic's in Flemington on occasion, and because we all sometimes attended Mass in Polish at Saint Vincent's church in Ashfield. As well as the Greek, Irish, Polish and Latvian influences, there were Italian shops and barbers, while on top of all this, St Brigid's parish church had a decidedly Spanish mission style. But for all that the ambience was decidedly Irish for this was Catholic Australia!

In the same street as the Catholic church was St Clement's Anglican church built in 1927 while around the corner was the Greek Orthodox church of Saint Nicholas of which it is written:

> The history of the St Nicholas Greek Orthodox Parish has its beginnings in the year 1961 when the first influx of Greek immigrants began settling in the Marrickville region. The Marrickville region had a great need for a church in the 1950s with thousands of migrant Greeks residing in the area. ... Between 1961 and 1966, the original house on the land acquired was converted into a church to be able to serve the Greek community of Marrickville and its surrounding regions with liturgies and sacraments. The church today is now performing sacraments to the 2nd and 3rd generation Greeks in the region.[9]

There was certainly a kind of verve to everyday life. The churches were often the focal point of the immigrants' identity. Weekend attendance at Sunday services gave a sense of community and continuity with the 'old country' and was often followed by get-togethers in the club of a particular group, and sometimes crossing over to others' groups. But the verve was interlaced with exhaustion as many worked long hours.

My parents worked extraordinary hours and seemed always tired. My father was employed in the British Leyland Factory in Zetland on the factory floor and as a budding manager, while my mother was a trainee doctor in her new language, English, at Marrickville Hospital, carrying out various assessments and exams. Strange to say, neither of these jobs yielded any large salary but there was just enough at the time to pay the mortgage, health bills and to help relations overseas. Yet these were halcyon years before my mother succumbed to various illnesses and could no longer work, meaning a reduced source of income. As my parents' jobs kept them away long hours, as happened and happens with many immigrants, I was left with my Babcia during the week who delighted me with her Polish singing and stories.

My father and mother, with my cousin Michael Kulic, the intrepid cowboy, and I.

Students at a Sydney primary schools sitting at typical mid C20 school desks, whether at government or Catholic schools. These desks had an attached shelf where pupils stored their earthly goods. Courtesy of J&J Dellit 'Lessons from the Past'. http://www.jdellit.com.au/2011/06/13/lessons-from-the-past-1/

Here are my cousins in Poland (circa 1958/9) who were growing up in Soviet controlled Poland with a sombre faced Santa Claus. Soviet leaders could not quite stamp out Santa Claus nor Polish Catholicism. Here are Janusz, Wojtek and Andrzej Tydda in Lublin (where my father was born) They heard about Uncle Stalin and Lenin regularly in class. We were to meet in later life.

A typical bottle of milk given daily to children by the government of that time. It was 1/3 of a pint and many remember the milk's sourness after it had been delivered and left in the hot Australian sun. But flavoured straws helped – at least at my school. The flavoured straw maker probably became a millionaire as the straws were so popular.

Looking at shops, free libraries and Aussie friends

With little or no spare money, migrants derived their enjoyment from looking at things in their spare time, as looking at things is free. On Saturdays my father took me to the local Marrickville library where we spent many happy hours reading books. We walked hand in hand talking about everything under the sun and then pored over books together in the quiet atmosphere of a 'books only' library. As well, I used to sit on the front porch of our little cream-coloured semi, and watch people go by, imagining life in the houses of the street. A terrace across the road caught my attention – I thought it would be wonderful to live in one, just to go up and down the stairs all day. Mostly I waited for my father to turn the corner down the street at the end of the long day and would run down the street to embrace him. He was so tired after a day's work, yet listened to *Children's Hour* with me on the ABC and sometimes the *Mickey Mouse Club*. My mother had shift hours so they changed all the time but I was always very happy when she returned. My mother, father, grandmother and I had some fun times in the small backyard where there was an outside 'dunny' hence one of the great achievements was to build an 'inside' toilet so there was less risk of encountering spiders in the loo.

An Aussie joins the family

Sitting on the porch one day I met an Australian girl (in the sense of sixth generation Aussie) passing by. Her name was Lorraine and she was around seven years of age. We got to talking and soon I found out that Lorraine lived with her family down the street in an old ramshackle, timber house. When I say ramshackle, this is almost too good a word. The walls sagged, the tin iron roof was rusty and had holes in it, and the 'house' had an earthen floor, the family renting it for a pittance. While our semi in Holmesdale Street was small, it had a floor and a roof. I had never seen anything like

Lorraine's house with its old beds with rusty metal frames spread here and there, on which most of the family slept. Lorraine was one of 10 children who lived there with an alcoholic father and overwrought mother. Standing on this earthen floor with my new friend, for the first time I saw bread and dripping. I said hello to the members of the family who were there, some sleeping and some awake. Soon afterwards, Lorraine came to my place and for the first time she saw salami and frankfurts, for my grandmother had found the place to buy these staples of any East European's life. As a Pole you could be poor as a church mouse, but with your last cents you would buy salami. An enterprising Pole called Kaczanowski had opened up some smallgoods places in Ashfield and sold smoked sausage and particularly salami to highly appreciative customers, who came from every corner of Sydney to get their 'kielbasa' (i.e., 'sausage'). Lorraine could not pronounce Kaczanowski or even my surname, but she definitely liked Polish sausage. Babcia was delighted and fed her as much as she wanted.

Lorraine came often to play hopscotch, chasings and 'dolls', apparently enjoying what must have seemed a strange migrant family. I recall her staring at us with her freckled face and ginger hair, bemused and puzzled at what she was experiencing. In fact, after sharing a lot of time with us, due to the irrepressible missionary efforts of my mother, Lorraine ended up becoming a Catholic. No-one in Lorraine's family seemed to mind her change of religion at all. I don't think they basically took too much notice – they may have been Anglicans but I am not sure. At Marrickville Public School, which she attended, she was suddenly put into Catholic Scripture classes. Lorraine then occasionally attended Mass at the Latvian Catholic church, as we called Saint Dominic's in Flemington, as well as at St Brigid's church. One day she joined a long line of Latvian flower girls welcoming a Sydney bishop at the Latvian church, and no-one noticed her ginger hair and freckles at all as she walked in procession, throwing handfuls of flower petals on the path, as girls did then. She enjoyed it immensely that she, an Aussie, was accepted as a Latvian.

Marrickville, the paprika king, salami sandwiches and pies

Apart from predominantly Greeks, Italians and long-term Aussies, there actually was someone from central Europe in Marrickville who became well known as the Paprika King:

> Vojtech Zimmer, born in Vienna, fled Austria at the beginning of World War II. He joined the free Czech forces but was torpedoed off Gibraltar. He then joined French forces in the south of France. At the evacuation of Dunkirk he became a British soldier. Zimmer arrived in Sydney in 1948 and took various factory jobs before establishing a company to sell Hungarian spices and condiments. The factory moved to Marrickville in the 1960s. Zimmer was affectionately known as the Paprika King, receiving in 1973 an Order of the British Empire.[10]

At the time I had no knowledge of the Paprika King but I did take along salami sandwiches to St Brigid's. This entailed some social humiliation as all those reffo children who ate salami sandwiches for lunch in the 60s will attest. While the post-war classes had migrant baby boomers, there were still plenty of 'dinky-di, eat a pie' Aussies there, and it was clear that their lunches were very different from mine. The very existence of salami on thick rye bread often elicited long suspicious stares, as if they were examining bombs or anthrax. These sandwiches had no delicate 'shaved' salami slices, as one has nowadays, but thick slabs of salami, thicker often than the bread, a sign of good post-war living to my parents, who yearned for this in the war years when they were so hungry. But to my Aussie peers it was 'urky purky' stuff and I was ostracised from the mainstream of second class life. Many other immigrant children had adapted to the peanut butter/ pie/ sausage roll eating playground culture but I was clearly a remedial learner and had a long way to go. What to do?

One evening at age six, I prevailed upon my grandmother to give me one shilling so I could buy a pie. She was a very kind grandmother and willingly gave me the shilling. So I came with great anticipation to school and ordered a pie from the small canteen. I was clearly now super cool and had become a true Australian.

I did not realise, however, that to be cool, it is not enough to buy a pie, one has to know how to eat it. Having a pie in my hands for the first time in my life, I proudly took it out of the brown paper bag. My fingers gripped the top rim of the pie with such gusto that the bottom part filled with meat spilled out onto the front of my uniform making a terrible mess. The onlookers ran away as this may have spelt trouble for them. A passing teacher exploded in anger and I was then berated for not even being able to eat a pie properly (which every true Australian could do). So I stood in utter humiliation and somehow realised I had a longer way to go. But I was determined to practise the arcane art of pie eating as much as I could, and so ordered more pies in the following weeks.

Finally, on one glorious day in Marrickville, whose exact date I cannot remember, I attained to the lofty height of success. I ate a whole pie without mishap, acquiring that pie-eating sophistication, that epitome of Aussie cool.

4

BABY BOOMERS, STRESS AND THE SACRAMENTS

Pies and salami aside, the central purpose of our education was to enter into Catholic culture, a world on its own which invisibly beckoned us all to its core. It so happened that St Brigid's was under the care of the Good Samaritan nuns and some lay teachers. The spiritual realm and the world of reading, writing and arithmetic unfolded in daily succession with church and school existing in a seamless union. At a very young age, these enormous classes of post-war Catholics in Marrickville were being prepared for the holiest of holy anchors of Catholic life, the Sacraments, which every Catholic child was to receive in second and third class – Confession and Holy Communion (and later Confirmation). And so began induction into the eternal realm.

We sat in class listening to instructions as to how we were to prepare for our first Confession. At age six, I had to examine my conscience over the entire span of my life and note every sin. We knew from the story of Adam and Eve that humanity was flawed and we were examples of this pervasive flawed human condition so we had to accuse ourselves of our moral weaknesses. We were utterly serious and in awe of being in the confessional, of coming before God for judgement and forgiveness. We knew God existed, the Ten Commandments existed, and that God was going to judge us according to them. This was the real world gradually being revealed to us. We all moved in unison to cross this heavenly Rubicon.

But in the end, we were just six or seven years old. I recall the long queue for my first Confession winding from Livingstone Road in Marrickville into the large white church, as we stood hands united in prayer. Some thought the greater number of sins they had, the better the confession would be. Some children said out loud in the queue, with traffic going by: 'How many sins have you got?' One girl answered: '50'. Another said: '80' and another, drawing gasps from us, saying, 'I've got 100! Some racked their brains to see if these totals could be matched. No-one could match 100 sins.

I recall the priest who prepared us having told us, at one stage, that we were not to confess the sin of 'adultery' as one boy had mistakenly done, as he had added water to the milk he bought for his mother after drinking half the bottle. This was 'adulterating' the milk and not the sin of adultery, the priest explained. I am surprised we could even understand such words at this tender age, but evidently we did. As we filed reverently into the dark, awe-inspiring church with statues of saints in shadows, and Jesus Himself in the confessional, we were prepared to lay our lives bare before God and try to become better people. I have no idea how the priest behind the grille heard the sincere recitation of all our sins but we were ushered in, one by one, to the confessional booths to tell them all and beg for God's mercy, then exiting sombrely to say our penances, and walking back in silence to our classes.

In this simple way, the spiritual legacy of the Catholic Church confronted the growing spirit of the age, the growing prevalence of humanistic psychology, popular at the time and the Frankfurt school anti-authoritarianism growing in America. For example humanist Carl Rogers, so 'hot' and popular at that time, insisted that there was no such thing as sin. What a historical irony that Rogers was lecturing to huge American university classes, to predominantly Christian audiences, at the very same time as we were making our first Confessions, very aware of the human tendency to sin.

Rogers insisted that human beings were basically good (and this after World War II!) and that there was no such thing as objective morality.[11] Rogers, in his highly popular work *On Becoming a Person* (1961), in attacking what he saw as an over-emphasis on guilt in the Christian legacy, attacked all sense of guilt. He stated confidently that the 'inmost core of man ... is positive' and that 'there is no beast in man. There is only man in man'.[12] And here at St Brigid's Marrickville, at the age of six, I was taught exactly the opposite, as had my entire generation of Catholic primary school students. The sense of guilt was not oppressive. It existed as a dramatic, sad acknowledgment of a flawed humanity, of which we saw ample evidence around us. If we were shocked by it, we were the same age as Jacinta of Fatima who was shown an actual vision of hell in the account of the apparitions in Portugal. But it depended on how it was conveyed. From a common sense point of view, it seemed quite reasonable to think human beings were not perfect and that they needed to work on themselves. It was certainly evident to those with East European parents who had witnessed the worst of horrors, about which they heard as they grew up. The human capacity for evil shocked me even more than the existence of hell.

We knew nothing of ideological wars being waged around us in humanistic psychology, existential philosophy, cultural Marxism or post-modern moral relativism. I doubt our teachers knew, or if they did, they believed in what they taught more. It was not until a decade later that Catholic psychologists began to critique this Rogerian view of guiltless human beings because it had become so influential. The savvy pioneer of such critique was US psychologist Paul Vitz. He saw how many fell under Rogers' sway and argued that the Rogerian notion of unconditional self-regard was 'completely at odds with the Christian doctrine of original sin', adding that the notion of the 'intrinsically good' self who can do no evil was a theory that 'has dominated much of American psychotherapy and much popular psychology and educational theory, from Rogerian therapy to Transactional Analysis'.[13] Vitz saw Rogerian abolition of guilt as utopian and dangerous. But what did we know, we little Catholics in the making, as we ate pies and went to church, about the momentous ideological shifts around us? We just knew human beings were flawed.

Title deeds to the church, a brief historic detour

The white, Spanish Mission style church in Marrickville, in which these first sacraments took place for us tiny children, was impressive with its Four Angels of the Apocalypse above the altar dome-canopy, and a plethora of saints and statues on every side. As Australian historian Edmund Campion said, 'Catholicism is the religion of the imagination which speaks to its people through their senses ... wax candles, rosary beads and medals and oil'.[14] The church certainly 'spoke' to us, in ways more eloquent than words, as we gazed around its meaningful symbols. Poor or rich, all students looked up and around its interior and felt it was theirs – an abiding symbol of 'belonging', especially important for lonely, deracinated refugees and migrants in post-war Australia. We were all culturally and spiritually rich in another way and owned the title deeds of the church and all it represented.

The church of St Brigid in Marrickville has certainly had an interesting history. This was not the original Catholic church in Marrickville. The first, established in 1886, was built in Despointes Street, not far from the current church, and was called 'St Brigid in the Fields'.[15] This was the name given by Cardinal Moran, who apparently vetoed the decision of Father Doyle (the first parish priest), who had wanted to call it the Church of the Holy Shroud. The Good Samaritan Sisters began teaching children in the church building in 1887 during the week, with the building being converted back to a church on the Sunday. The Good Samaritans

Marrickville's St Brigid's school and very impressive Spanish mission style church which still retains most of its original features today. Here my class was prepared for our first Confession and Holy Communion.

Above the altar we regularly looked on, was a canopy with the Four Angels of the Apocalypse blowing trumpets to announce the end of the world.

We were surrounded by statues and pictures in churches in the 1960s. These made a deep impression on us as a 'silent' catechesis. Here in St Brigid's church, Marrickville, is St Paul of the Cross (1694-1775), founder of the Passionists who ran the parish in the 1960s.

This was St Brigid's school as I remember it in the 1960s. I was in 2nd class in the room to the left of the centre entrance on the ground floor, taught by Miss Deane with 45 in the class (there were two second classes). In 3rd class, we were taught by Sr Ambrosine with 57 in the class.

Procession in the grounds of St Brigid's church Marrickville circa 1957, not long before I arrived there. It is most likely a procession in honour of St Maria Goretti who had died a martyr's death. She had been canonised in 1950 and was a very popular saint.

Procession in honour of St Maria Goretti, circa 1957, with students of the Good Samaritans in processions with palms, the symbol of martyrdom.

A good Samaritan nun, Sister Helena Eksa, whose parents were post-war Latvian refugees in Australia. She did much community work and has since passed away but I had the privilege of meeting her.

The old Good Samaritan Convent was located for a time in Marrickville, in this building called 'Malakoff Towers', which has since been demolished and is now the site of Marrickville Police Station.

A typical first Holy Communion dress worn by Catholic girls in the 1950s and 60s. Here is Robyn Tandy on her first Communion day in 1956. Note the rosary and prayer book in her hands.

Here I sit in 1960, with the sun in my eyes, to the right of the Sydney Latvian priest, Fr Gaidelis, in Holy Communion dress at St Dominic's, Flemington, Sydney. Those of Latvian background came after their actual first Holy Communion in parish churches to show the Latvian community we had reached this milestone.

Flower girls casting petals before a visiting bishop near the Latvian church of St Dominic in Flemington (Sydney) around 1960. My Aussie friend Lorraine, a recent convert (at the front) was pleased to be a Latvian flower girl and wore her first Holy Communion dress for the occasion.

First Communion day for Marita Cudmore in the 1970s who attended St Kevin's Catholic school in Eastwood, Sydney. The dress lengths had gone up though the solemnity of the day was paramount.

A group of girls on their first Holy Communion day in the 1970s from St Kevin's in Eastwood.

A typical group of boys in their first Holy Communion attire in the 1960s, wearing their special medals.

Peter Macinante on his first Communion day with prayer book and medal in the early 1960s and a happy Damien Cudmore on his first Communion day in 1967.

A group of First Holy Communicants from St Brigid's School, Marrickville, mid 1950s (Reprinted with permission).

of Saint Benedict had been working in Australia for a long time by the time I encountered them. They constituted the first institute of religious women formed in Australia, established by Archbishop Polding in 1857. Until 1866 the sisters were called Good Shepherd Sisters but the title was changed to avoid confusion with an older order of the same name. Their first temporary home was on the corner of Petersham and Marrickville Roads where, apparently, a Chinese restaurant now stands. However as time went on, plans for a grander church were made. It was the era of sectarianism, and not easy to buy land at the time but it was finally purchased in 1915:

> ... by a middle man because of the anti-Catholic bigotry of the owners. Fr. Alphonsus Cohen CP was called from Goulburn in 1915 to be Superior and Parish Priest. His task was to pay off the £17,500 debt on the new property and to begin the enormous task of planning and fund raising for the new church. It was the middle of the Great War.[16]

The Passionist order of priests, who had arrived in 1877, had been asked to take on the parish. From 1903-1911 the population of Marrickville had grown enormously from farm lands to become a growing suburb on the edge of Sydney. A new, bigger church was needed so a grand church was built through the efforts of the community on the corner of Marrickville and Livingstone Roads named simply 'St Brigid's'. Passionist priest Fr. Alphonsus Cohen CP was called from Goulburn in 1915 to be Superior and Parish Priest and faced the mammoth task of dealing with the £17,500 debt on the new property and to begin the enormous task of planning and fund raising for the new church. After the establishment of the church, a website history notes that 'Fr. Alphonsus died of exhaustion in the Little Company of Mary Hospital at Lewisham in 1917', just before the foundation stone was laid and blessed in that same year.¹⁷ The same source says of the grand dome over the sanctuary:

> The overlapping leaf pattern on the top of the Tabernacle is repeated in the great dome over the baldachino, in the Sanctuary lamps and more recently in the newly commissioned top of the Baptismal font (made by De Metz, a traditional Italian firm). The architectural style is known as Spanish Mission. The Church is one metre shorter than St. Mary's, Concord, but holding more people it is, after the cathedral itself, the biggest Church in the Sydney Archdiocese.¹⁸

This church into which we little children entered, as if it belonged to us, was already a 'national shrine' replete with reference to the Passion of Christ:

> The church was built as a National Shrine for the Passion and references to the Passion and to the Passionists can be found written everywhere into the decoration of the church. There are the great statues of the Ecce Homo, Our Lady of Sorrows and the Pieta. These priceless statues were carved in Italy from Carrara marble. ... The Great Rose Window features symbols of the Passion: Cross, crown of thorns, the Cock, the Scourging Pillar, Spear and Hyssop Stick, and the Passionist Sign in the centre. Towards the front of the church there are a number of round sandstone medallions above the pews. These also feature the signs and symbols of the Passion, this time including the Eucharist itself by which the Passion of Jesus is made present again sacramentally. Incidentally above these medallions are four large square panels that show the symbols of the Four Evangelists, the Lion (St. Mark), the Ox (St Luke), the Eagle (St. John) the Scribe (St. Matthew).

Not knowing all these details, the inner message and traditional symbols wove its way into our hearts, minds and consciousness.

Moreover, it is interesting to note that after the post-Vatican II changes in many churches, when statues were removed and high altars destroyed, most at St Brigid's remained intact:

> The High Altar with its relief of Leonard da Vinci's Last Supper was not moved after the Vatican Council II. It has always stood beneath the soaring Baldachino with its rich mosaics and trumpeting angels.[19]

Totally unaware of any of this illustrious past history, nor of revolutions to come, when I entered the church as a six-year-old girl in long plaits with my two front milk teeth missing, I felt I had entered eternity and that it would always be there. It is so powerful to sense the sacred, to 'sense eternity' as a child – for it never leaves you. We children would always gaze silently at the statues of angels, and up at the ceiling, and had no doubt the church had been there from the beginning of time. Of immense significance, above all, was the reality of God's presence, the church's bigness seeming to confirm it and so our souls were touched again and again. We may as well have been in St Peter's Basilica, Santa Maria Maggiore, San Giovanni in Laternano, Santa Maria in Trastevere, or in any grand church in Rome. Without knowing many details, the Western Judeo-Christian inheritance was being transmitted to us powerfully in St Brigid's Marrickville, in art work, buildings, prayer, gestures, insistence on reverence and the liturgy. There was an authentic sense of the sacred whose transmission worked powerfully and continually on toothless six-year old-Wanda and her classmates.

Domine non sum dignus

As I recall, we visited the church often. Having confessed our sins, we were then prepared with great seriousness for our First Holy Communion. On that day, girls put on their white dresses and veils, boys were in suits and ties, if they had them, the Greek and Italian tailors on Marrickville Road doing a roaring trade. We knew how to enter the church in utter silence, we recognised the words at the opening of the Mass and knew that 'Kyrie Eleison' meant 'Lord have mercy' in Greek even though we were six and seven years old. We held the palms of our hands together and bowed our heads at the Consecration, when Jesus came to us.

As Holy Communion approached, we said the 'Domine non sum dignus' ('Lord I am not worthy') together, all knowing we were unworthy of the sacrament. It was not just a question of saying the words, it was the deep absorption of that spiritual territory which became the foundation of the Catholic legacy we were inheriting. We were imbued with awe and all utterly terrified lest we offended Heaven by not kneeling properly, not swallowing the Sacred Host on time, or not returning to our pews without falling over in the crowded church. Heads down, hands together, I remember the slow steps up the aisle to the altar rails, kneeling in anticipation, receiving the Communion Host on the tongue and walking back to the pews solemnly, as we had been taught to do. We understood the words: 'Corpus Domini nostri Jesu Christi custodiat animam tuam in vitam aeternam. Amen.' ('May the Body of our Lord Jesus Christ preserve your soul unto life everlasting. Amen') without any difficulty at all. No-one who has not been through it could imagine the drama of the priest approaching with the chalice, ready to place the host on our tongues, for the first time, with the altar boy holding the golden paten, the moment of receiving Holy Communion, and moving on after the momentous event takes place. I thought that the church would totally explode in some way, at this very moment, or that I would be whisked off to another planet never to return, but that was just a childish way of imagining this great internal change in our lives. Making sure not to fall over, now united with God, we were to walk back slowly to the pews, despite shaking, knobbly knees, and we were to kneel and bend over to thank Our Lord for the greatest gift of all time, and presumably never to rise up from this position again.

We were taught that Holy Communion was the apex of our lives and henceforth nothing would be the same. This was an extraordinary experience for six- and seven-year-olds who pinched, punched and giggled as much as anyone at that age in the playground and who, at other times, sang the hymns 'Pange Lingua' and 'Sweet Sacrament Divine' in the filled to capacity church. While I do not seem to have any photos of the day, like many children, moments and scenes of it are engraved in my memory, and in speaking to contemporaries who still have photos, they seem fairly typical as for any child who received First Holy Communion during this era. My friend Rod Pyne particularly recalls the nun who prepared him for his First Holy Communion, Mother Eymard, who told the class that this would be the best day of their lives and Rod recalls that indeed it was. Rod still has his Holy Communion medal, and like many others who went through Catholic schools, has nothing but positive, poignant memories of the day. Another friend Peter Macinante recalls his first Communion Day at St Declan's in Penshurst in similar vein being dressed in the finest clothes. Catholic children, however young, could rarely forget this spiritual milestone.

Ongoing induction into the eternal present

With the inauguration of the Sacraments, that unique blend of the spiritual and temporal was henceforth woven ever more strongly into every young Catholic's life. We learned our prayers, recited them in class, knew the rosary and attended Mass at the church next door in the midst of statues, pictures and incense, as if this was the most normal thing in the world to do. This was our story, the rich spiritual genealogy of us all. Whether Chinese or Irish we were transformed and entered another world of divine, moral parameters.

It was more than icing on an educational cake for it threaded all we did with a vision of time and eternity. Many who lived through this era will know what I mean. It was not one event, one thing, or one prayer. It was a spiritual sensibility permeating each day, transmitted to those who had lived here for generations, and to the more recent immigrants and 'reffos' who just adapted to its universality and felt grounded and secure within it. It was a spiritual and social milieu of 'lush hymns and flowering prayers' as Edmund Campion put it, that sank deep into our life narrative.[20] It united us. It came with and without words, in forms of art and formless moments of being, sparks from the deep and ethereal beyond. It came through what Paul Connerton refers to as the passing on of tradition in 'non-textual and non-cognitive ways', making explicit the assumed spiritual and cultural structure of our world.[21] The solid church with its plethora of beauty, in image and Scriptural reference, united all the fragments of life, every kind of human person, every suffering, every joy, not only making sense, but anchoring our existence in whatever chaos our lives may have held.

How extraordinary that this precious legacy was conveyed to us before the age of eight, traditionally taken to be 'the age of reason'. And while it was conveyed in 1960, as I said earlier, I would not have had a clue what the words 'Vatican II' meant, though at that very same time, it was obviously being planned in Rome. I had no clue who Bob Santamaria was, who at that very time saw Australia as threatened by Communist unions, and had acted politically and split the Labor Party. Nor did my parents know. But I knew what being a Catholic was and that somehow I, and the students in my class, personally owned the Spanish Mission style church at St Brigid's.

The reffo kid acquires Irish blarney

In fact, this spiritual inheritance was much easier to understand than my immediate family genealogy, at least on my mother's side. I would often be politely asked where I came from, or where my parents came from. Hardly any Australian knew where Latvia was, it being such a small country and unfamiliar to Marrickvillians. I would get flustered and could not explain where it was. I could explain 'Poland' easily but would hesitate to answer about my mother's Latvian background as I knew the strange response I would get from saying the word 'Latvia'. If only I could say I was Greek, Maltese or Italian, things would have been so much easier.

One day, when asked by a teacher where my mother came from, I decided not to say Latvia. We were outside the church and I said, shamelessly, at age 7, that my mother came 'from where they speak Latin'. As we all were using Latin in our daily prayers and lives, it seemed to me Latin was not a dead language at all but very much alive. I remember clearly trying to spin this yarn, explaining to the skeptical teacher that my mother spoke Latin at home. While it was true my mother spoke some Latin as she attended Mass, she spoke Latvian, English, German and Polish at home, as was needed, but this was another matter altogether. I was disappointed my teacher did not believe me. My imaginative account of our ancient Roman roots just could have been true if she had taken a longer view of history. But, after this failed attempt, I saw that people did not take easily to being told one came from ancient Rome. I quickly saw through the error of my ways in spinning such a yarn and realised Latin was a dead language for most people. My efforts in explaining the Latvian background of my mother, though heroic, were doomed and I continued to say 'Latvian' and be considered incomprehensible. But I had acquired my Irish blarney certificate.

A group of First Holy Communion children, from Holy Cross School, Daylesford, Victoria, circa 1950s?
(Reprinted with permission).

At his post Communion 'party', Damien Cudmore with his classmates in 1967 and (right) a First Holy Communion Certificate from Our Lady Star of the Sea parish, Watsons Bay, in the 1940s.

5

CHANGE AND STABILITY
IN THE MIDST OF SADNESS

While life went ever forward and upward for many immigrants and reffos, there were many who buckled under the stresses and strains of post-war life. People like to tell success stories of migrants – 'He came with a suitcase and became a billionaire' and such type of tale. The reality was there were many who came and lived under the cloud of the horrors they experienced during the war and many tended to keep their sadnesses and failures to themselves. No billionaire stories here, just survival.

These years in Marrickville, despite their colourful aspects, became, in fact, a very sad time for all of us. After these two years of hard work, everything became too much; the family broke down and my parents separated. There was no question of 'others' involved or the usual scenarios; it was a question of things falling apart. It was the saddest event of my life – for them and myself – as for many children in a similar situation. I never really understood it at the time but I see it, from the distance of years, as not being anyone's 'fault'. There was no fault, but as with many post-war refugees, it was enmeshed in a wider canvas, the longer term consequences of war. Though these are not reasons, they are perhaps contributing factors. My mother survived several bomb blasts and never saw her family again after 18, while my father was shot many times, losing all his classmates in the Warsaw Uprising; and added to these the relentless, immense pressures on both, social and psychological. From childhood I had felt a protective instinct towards both parents, truly deserving of a compassion and understanding which they could not find around them. They were both beautiful people, with deep, generous hearts, and yes, they survived, and many have endured worse, but as most realise, people are different in the way they handle life's experiences, especially when that involves war and traumatic stress. Any family break-up is profound in its effects on all involved. I recall the beginnings of a sense of tragedy being threaded into my life, a formless, almost wordless sadness in a territory all its own.

For many years afterwards, I saw many similar sad situations. This is the 'other side' of typical migrant stories. People prefer good news stories with few wanting to hear of those who went quietly mad, lived in penury, took to drink, did not become rich, or lived and died in loneliness. I heard many such stories. Post-war survivors are fortunate if they can survive as a family unit for that is a solid base for co-operation and a future life in a new land. Many don't make it, and, as I said, it is not a question of blame: war and displacement have their own dynamic and complex effects for years, and there are too many threads to unravel. Things can fall apart. Some grow up in the shadow of many kinds and layers of grief, the 'survivors' not being in any sense better than those who buckled. The first generation of war and holocaust survivors, whatever their backgrounds, know this only too well and I felt great understanding from some Jewish friends I met later in life.

While it is not my intention to dwell on these events, as that would constitute a separate story, it is enough to note that they happened. What is important is that they happened precisely in the context of the type of Catholic education I was receiving at the time. The sacraments and the Catholic school provided a deeply embedded stability, a 'still point in the turning world', the reality of God's mercy and love. This was a continual balm. Of course all schools can provide stability to children in breaking families but this was stability with a difference. Strangely, I was aware that beneath the loss of our previous life, there was an eternally present world that would never disappear and in retrospect, what a consolation and grounding this reality provided for me in the days to come. It made sense. My known world may have disappeared but I had a place in the world, all had a place in it.

No matter how many criticise it, the Catholic culture was and is an immense buffer against the upheavals of a broken home and the aftermath of war. I'm sure there are others who can say this of their school years. I was more fortunate than many children in such situations in that my parents were thoughtful and kind. They remained in contact with each other and I in turn was constantly in touch with them. My grandmother was close to both and saw things in a wider perspective. So I always had both parents, my grandmother, aunts and uncles and other relations and was always visiting someone or another.

I was becoming aware, however, even if only from a child's perspective, of how the past influences the present, threading it in all kinds of unexpected ways. I once saw a great-aunt crying alone in a chicken coop in the backyard of her family's home, whisky bottle beside her, missing all she had lost in Latvia. My grandmother, genial as she was, would almost shake when shown sweet potato, for this had been her staple diet in the concentration camp. Things simmered ... forgetfulness was sought for but did not always come. I was aware of silences, reflective gazes, of people feeling too emotionally overwhelmed to talk about camps and gulags, when asked. For this involved family members. My great-uncle was in a gulag. Another great uncle spent years running from both Nazis and Soviets to evade camps and gulags (and survived). I was to learn my Latvian grandfather was likely murdered by the Soviets. We knew of many who had been in concentration camps and I met them all throughout my childhood. In this way, I was immersed in the shadows of another world, another 'inherited' story, and even experienced some beginnings of 'survivor guilt'. This probably accounts for my nascent interest in observing people, thinking about them, their resilience in war and peace, how families continue after trauma and falling apart, and my becoming a psychologist years later.

Moving away from Marrickville

After two years in Marrickville, a new family situation evolved. We all moved again but in different directions. While my mother and I moved to live in rented rooms in a terrace house surgery in Paddington, my father and grandmother lived in rented rooms in Darlinghurst, close to their city-based work. So I had new experiences in other parts of Sydney and, while sad at the loss of a former world, my attention was drawn to observe and remember the panoply of events which surrounded us in the inner city.

In fact, Paddington and Darlinghurst were interesting places – especially before their later gentrification – and we lived there when these places were much poorer and had many 'characters' as residents. They were close to the city so I got to know the streets well and became part of the scenario of 'characters': the street sellers, old time Paddo residents, the cat lady, war wounded, those who remembered the Depression and the sense of class wars. My father came on weekends and took me for walks or to movies –at St James, the Paris, the Capitol and other wonderful Sydney cinemas – where mostly we sat in the 'Stalls' but occasionally ventured into the 'Lounge' or 'Dress Circle' area. What a journey around the world this was. We also went to the Museum and from this I recall my father's interest 'in everything': 'Wandy, why do sparrows eat several times their weight in food every day?', he would ask, and then proceed to unfurl this mystery as if the world's existence depended on it. My mother took me to Centennial Park and we fed the rather well built ducks there. We had good times and continued to do things that migrants did for free: walk around parks, feed the birds, visit libraries, or go to our ethnic community groups; but going to movies sometimes was added as an highly desirable 'extra'. I have such piquant memories of Sydney in the 1960s: seeing the Cat Lady feeding dozens of cats in laneways, watching Anzac Day parades, double-decker buses, the trips to Luna Park and the Zoo, newspaper stands, street kiosks, Greek hamburger shops, fish and chips wrapped in newspaper and fairy floss at Circular Quay.

This was the era when the Easter Show was in Moore Park. I recall vividly the show bag and doll on a stick of which I was once the proud owner. Sitting on the top deck of the bus, we observed the conductor, passengers and Oxford Street, with its old, jaded buildings, its contrasting noble town hall, seeing streets of endless terrace houses with rusting iron lace balconies, many smelling of leaking gas and musty furniture before Paddington acquired any higher reputation. Another great excitement for my father and myself was watching the froth build up in a glass of Coca Cola.

The rhythm of life on the streets of old Paddo and Darlo also inevitably became threaded with our Catholic identity. This meant visiting their respective churches, which I did with both parents – not to mention the Polish and Latvian churches. All this assuaged the sorrows of living in a 'broken family', for we were always going somewhere. Somehow the eternal realities of the Catholic world placed the inevitable tragedies of this world in another eternally surrounding perspective. The panoply of life in the back streets and lanes offered great interest and colourful episodes. My mother and I lived in rented rooms on Oxford Street, above a medical surgery where she worked as an assistant doctor, making visits at night to grateful patients. These were the years when her health was still reasonable, but the hours of work were unreasonable. She was often called out at night, three or four times (as well as carrying out day work), so the secretary of the surgery, who also rented a room upstairs in the surgery, would be my 'guardian'. Across the road from where we lived was the Greek hamburger shop and Joe's fruit palace, not to mention an old style Coles, with its tantalising open displays of purses for 1/6d and a whole range of items one could ogle at but not buy. In the back lanes I connected with neighbourhood children, like Maria the Greek girl who played hopscotch with me. Then there were Julie and Cathy, who lived in a very old timber Paddington house which they rented, and whose family my mother converted to Catholicism after a few visits. Lorraine, another one of my mother's converts from Marrickville, came to visit from time to time and we had great fun. But looming over all of this was the church next door, St Francis, and its reminder of the eternal cosmos, just a few steps away. In retrospect, it was for me like living in a monastery as a child as I saw the groups of daily Mass attenders come and go in the church to their regular pews, missals in hand. I was used to seeing multiple Masses proceed at the same time at side altars each day as happened in those times. But once having arrived in Paddington, I had to enrol in another Catholic school. Where to go now?

6

COOGEE, MOTHER PASCAL AND A NEW DUTCH IDENTITY

After the two years at St Brigid's, Marrickville, I was duly re-enrolled into my first St Brigid's, Coogee, again, for continuity's sake, as I had been there in kindergarten. While it was not the nearest school, and was a bus ride away from Paddington, my parents thought I could manage it as I was growing up –already in fourth class! People did not worry much about kidnapping, paedophiles or terrorism in that era, so I was taken to Anzac Parade each morning, and went by the bus 373 or 372 to school. Travelling by bus had entertaining aspects and interesting characters, like Bea Miles the Shakespeare-quoter who travelled free of charge on all Sydney buses. I saw her once hitting a bus with her umbrella as the conductor had upset her asking for a ticket. She alighted in a huff between bus stops, the driver being only too happy to stop for her to let her off. I had a wonderful time with my official School Bus Pass, with bus conductors maintaining civil order on the single and double deckers, people reading newspapers over each others' shoulders, and seeing open vistas from the top deck front seat. There was the mounting excitement of travelling to and from school, especially entering Carr Street in Coogee, seeing the sea in the distance, like a heavenly apparition, and entering a tunnel before reaching my bus stop, near the shop that sold ice blocks for fourpence, near which was the school. I apologise for so many food references in this story, but that is what preoccupied many of us students at the time: we saw buildings in terms of their potential to provide pies, chips and ice-blocks, that is, if we happened to have any pennies.

At St Brigid's, Coogee, no-one remembered me and, in any case, my world had become sadder and I was quieter. I was taller, looked different, had all my teeth, and my mother accompanied me in my box-pleated uniform on the first day. I spoke little with other students, sat and observed and adapted to the subjects being studied. Many children from broken families can understand this prolonged 'mourning'. But somehow the Catholic school had its own dynamism, charm, zaniness, character and sense of purpose that drew all like a magnet and took over. It enveloped and absorbed all who entered it. I may have changed houses but the eternal present surrounded me still and St Brigid's church at Coogee was yet another branch of it, to which I, the inheritor, had the title deeds.

I quickly turned to the most pressing issue of the moment and tried to understand what the teachers were saying to us. Some of the great topics of my fourth class education, which loom large in my memory, were 'The Mystery of the Inland Rivers' and 'The Crossing of the Blue Mountains'. Whatever Charlemagne may have meant to Western Europe, it was Blaxland, Lawson and Wentworth who were the decisive historical figures here! And we spent so much time studying this 'Mystery of the Inland Rivers' it is ironic that I don't today recall what the mystery was, nor what the answer was, just that there was a Mystery and it was so important to Australian history, to all existence itself. We spent months pondering, drawing and writing about the crossing of the Blue Mountains and frankly, I thought that there was no other mountain crossing in the world that would ever compare with it. We were all proud that Blaxland, Lawson and Wentworth had opened up Australia as it appeared to us they had opened up the entire globe. This was world history!

We also learned that Mount Koscziuszko was the highest mountain in Australia. Now being the child of a Polish refugee, I could say 'Koscziuszko' as a Pole would say it, which is very different from the way our Aussie teacher Mother Valerian pronounced it.

When she asked: 'Girls, what is the tallest mountain in Australia?', I raised my hand and said in a broad Aussie drawl 'Mount Koz-y-os-ko' in an Aussie accent, to her evident pleasure. This was not the place to insist on the Polish way of saying consonants.

Among the dedicated Brigidine nuns who taught us, I recall especially Mother Pascal, who with a leg disabled from polio, was principal and teacher of senior primary classes. She was an outstanding teacher and made her presence known by the stomping of her stick on the ground as she walked. One day, she stopped me along a walkway at school, and asked me to remind her what my background was. I had dropped all attempts to say I was descended from the inhabitants of ancient Rome, so in my shyness I said 'Poland', thinking my father's ancestry was easier to understand. But this created further problems. She heard this as 'Holland' so I was championed as 'that new Dutch girl' for quite a while, for I did not dare correct her. No-one corrected Mother Pascal, who had the status of an archangel, was a transmitter of the supernatural, who exuded presence, drama, immense knowledge, and who probably knew the Pope in Rome personally and certainly spoke with papal authority.

Order, Raffles and Grammar

One of the assumed realities of our lives in 4th class was that there was an order or discipline that should exist from one day to the next. We walked in ordered lines, two by two; we waited patiently in queues at the tuck shop; we walked up one side of the stairs; we were silent in St Brigid's church; did ordered steps in gymnastics and Irish dancing; we attended the Annual Fete and thought the Pope himself had invented Tombola, if not the Perpetual Raffle, a mainstay of parochial school fund raising; we had a fear of God, though I believe not an undue one; we knew there was a past, a present and a future; we knew this life was transitory and that there was a Last Judgement. We brought our fees to school each week – I carried two shillings and sixpence in an envelope to hand in on Monday. If you looked 'sensible', Mother Pascal would pick you to walk to the Commonwealth Bank with a black and gold money box with the total school fee takings for that week, to hand the bank teller with a note. No fear, no worries, we children felt so lucky to be picked to walk to the bank in Brook Street, always walking slowly back to school, to make the pleasure last longer.

With the sadder changes of family circumstances, as I started to get older, certain questions always nagged me: Would I ever make it through school? Would I get to the finishing line? Would things fall apart? Was there hope for me? Would I, a reffo kid, with a fractured biography, ever make it? It seemed such a long road then.

We did not see it as such then, but looking back I can see how easily we all adapted to the teaching style of the 1960s, with its rote learning and established verities of this life and the next, which could be referred to any time. This established some kind of stable pattern of learning, and no doubt a degree of emotional security. It seems quaint, and perhaps humorous in retrospect, but it worked on a profound level, in terms of its goals. We became very literate, so the world of books was opened to us. We could spell long words like 'Parramatta' and 'Tumburumba' with ease as we covered long spelling lists each day. We also engaged in that highly regarded, very serious activity which many school children were taught in that era, 'Parsing'. This meant analysing words in sentences grammatically. Mother Pascal, like a sergeant at a military parade, tapped a stick as we parsed words grammatically, day after day, like this:

> Mother Pascal (directs, loudly), 'Listen to this sentence! The woman read the book. Girls, parse the word "woman"!' Class replies (loudly) in unison, '"Woman"! Common noun, third person, singular number, feminine gender, subject to the verb "read".'

Then would come another word to parse, then another, then another. This went on for hours. Mother Pascal could tell with uncanny accuracy if you were not pulling your weight and just mouthing words silently. No-one was exempt. And heaven help you if you did not know the difference between a noun phrase, adverbial phrase and a clause. This was a grammatical crime. We engaged fervently in this kind of grammatical 'divine office' which we bellowed out daily and which we were certain would unfold the hidden secrets of the universe. I thought all mature adults parsed words at any time of night or day, as a rite of passage towards their maturity. I imagined universities must be full of adults who could parse the most difficult words with ease. Hoping for a happier future, I parsed my words fervently.

Pens, poetry and song

After hours of such grammatical incantation, like the monks singing the office at Solesmes, picking up a pen to write something was a huge change and indeed, excitement. We sat at old wooden desks – I'm sure many reading this know exactly the kind of desk I mean. These desks had a shelf beneath for books and technological equipment. I say 'technological' as in the mid-1960s we primary students thought we were at the cutting edge of modernity when we graduated from nib pens to using fountain pens. A lingering sense remained, however, that writing with a nib pen remained morally superior just because it took more effort, or so Mother Pascal argued. So it was with some vague sense of failure and resignation that fountain pens were finally introduced to us as the inevitable march of progress. But never, never would we accept ball point pens, evidence of sheer sloth and moral turpitude. To that dark place, none of us would venture. With pride, I would pull the little steel flap to draw ink, repeatedly, staring at my first fountain pen which I thought wonderful and which I was certain would last forever.

We strained and concentrated to write without blots, for writing was a serious business in this era, with a fountain pen as principal weapon and with ink as lifeblood – Quink Ink or Ancol, whichever was available. We filled our pens at home or at school like neurosurgeons preparing for a complex operation on the spine. Our task was to write neatly in 'running writing' on the lines of the page before us, as we were now on lofty heights beyond mere printing. If you wrote nice cursive writing without making blots on your page, you would be rewarded with a piece of blotting paper from Mother Pascal, which we all longed for, as for as a priceless treasure. You counted your pieces of blotting paper carefully as oligarchs might count their millions. You guarded them and felt so 'rich' that nothing else could match possessing them. If you blotted your page, you were told it looked like a spider had been sick on the page, and exhorted to see the error of your ways. Moral turpitude extended to being a persistent, recalcitrant page blotter. To this day I cannot see blotting paper without remembering this, nor the hankerings we all had for a piece of this paper treasure.

Inevitably, however, we did use ball point pens in years to come, but it was with some sense of great regret, some sense of a slackening world, of things going to pieces in some unaccountable way. And we were right, the world was going to pieces culturally, politically and morally in many ways but we did not quite understand this. We merely gleaned pieces of news from TV now and then, convinced that Mother Pascal was right about decadence deriving from ball point pens, even though we had a sneaking liking for them.

For a reffo kid who spoke no English on beginning school, I sure made up for it by enjoying reading and writing in English throughout my school years. We recited the poetry of Banjo Patterson, Dorothea Mackellar and Henry Kendall; there was a sense of pride in Australia's writers, especially her poets. I vividly recall the class chanting, in high pitched tones which sounded like

England's Westminster Cathedral (left), on which design the church of St Brigid's in Coogee was based, and St Brigid's parish church (right) as it stands today.

On my Confirmation day at St Brigid's, Coogee. I was very impressed with St Agnes so took this as a Confirmation name. Here I am with my grandmother in my confirmation dress with St Brigid's school in the background.

While I have no group photos of my primary school years, these are typical uniforms worn by many primary school children in the 1950s and 60s. This is 4th class at Prouille Dominican Primary School in Wahroonga with friend Robyn Tandy in the centre of the middle row.

These children at St Joseph's Catholic School in Rockdale are wearing typical school uniforms of the day.

Mother Pascal, vibrant teacher given to a Gaelic turn of phrase, who was also school principal at St Brigid's when I was there in the early 1960s. She taught a combined 5th and 6th class and directed many hours of grammatical parsing. (Right) Though considered 'new' in the 1960s, this hymnal had many old lush emotional religious hymns which we knew from memory, such as 'O Jesus Heart all burning, with fervent love for men ...'.

We were all told about the necessity of wearing a scapular and of wearing medals such as the Miraculous Medal and St Benedict Medals displayed here. (Right) As a Catholic you could become a member of the Propagation of the Faith society and here is a surviving card, typical of the era.

A Corpus Christi procession in 1967 up the road from St Brigid's, at Brigidine Convent School which I attended, being part of many such processions. There were many altar boys, girls in white dresses, uniforms, nuns, priests, singing and prayers.

Catholics were strongly urged to pray the rosary so school children were familiar with it. Here is my grandmother's rosary which I have to this day. (Right) Typical holy cards greatly desired by children of this era.

some forest bird chant, Kendall's poem 'Bell-Birds', in unison with the regular beat of an imaginary drum:

> By channels of coolness the echoes are calling,
> And down the dim gorges I hear the creek falling:
> It lives in the mountain where moss and the sedges
> Touch with their beauty the banks and the ledges.
> Through breaks of the cedar and sycamore bowers
> Struggles the light that is love to the flowers;
> And, softer than slumber, and sweeter than singing,
> The notes of the bell-birds are running and ringing.

I imagined the 'dim gorges' and 'moss and the sedges' as something wonderful I would set eyes on one day. I had as yet no idea what they meant. Words had an effect on me, even words I did not understand, as they pointed to a mystery into which I would delve ever deeper in my life. Our class read the widely distributed *School Magazine* and we all wrote stories. I recall a moment in fifth class, where the world stopped and I realised how much I loved words, long, short, funny or complex, and would seek unusual words in the dictionary with which to surprise Mother Pascal. I'm afraid I came out with lots of drivel such as 'The lugubrious looking boy sauntered dejectedly to the mysterious forest', which probably drove Mother Pascal crazy. If her cause for sainthood arises, I will be the first to extol her heroic patience in putting up with the verbal assassination of the English language of which I was guilty in fifth class.

Brazen articles, galootes and Johnny O'Keefe

We were persistently told: 'Keep your wits about you girls!' I imagined some kind of invisible presence called 'wits' which we should pull towards ourselves as often as possible to stay smart against a hostile world. Wits would help us, if only we had them whenever we needed them. If we did not behave well, we were called 'brazen articles' and 'galootes' by Mother Pascal – the latter being a Gaelic word which I did not understand at first, but sensed it meant someone not terribly good. And no-one wanted to be a galoote! Also we tried to avoid being called 'flibbertigibbets' (an old word of Middle English origin) which also signified moral failing. We were not to be a 'jellyfish' either, as we were expected to acquire backbones This expression, 'Don't be a jellyfish', which indicated moral crassness, persisted all through primary and high school. Another expression of the era was 'Girls, stop rooting around in your desks', an Irish idiomatic expression which rang in our innocent ears as an example of undesirable behaviour, meaning we should stop bending over to the shelf below our old desks and sit upright. Given time, we might have ended up speaking Gaelic as well as Latin!

A friend of mine recalls the boys in his primary class being told to avoid the 'lunatic fringe' who were always out to get you – a vivid image of all kinds of ever-present monsters in everyday life. During the 1960s another friend of Hungarian background, Gerard, recalls being told by teachers at Our Lady of the Rosary School in Fairfield, not only to avoid the lunatic fringe but not to be an 'Egypt', which is the way he heard it. 'Don't be an Egypt!' It seemed bad, whatever it was – a verity he was to believe in. However, he did not know what it meant, but coming from a teacher it sounded authoritative. But why, he wondered, were the people of Egypt associated with this sort of badness? This expression was used for years and it became a constant in his life. It was actually 'Don't be an idjut' (i.e., an idiot). But for years he wondered why he should not be an 'Egypt', until someone explained it to him, and the people of Egypt were exonerated from this incomprehensible guilt.

However, there was an expression directed at me sometimes. I could not avoid being called a 'useless article' as my practical skills were not so good. My help of others often made things worse. In fact I was a bit of a day-dreamer and always have been. But being a 'useless article' was not as bad as being a 'brazen article' – that was the pits. I took hope from never being labelled the latter, for coming from Mother Pascal in a severe, negative way, it clearly denoted a kind of moral deficiency from which one could only extricate oneself with the greatest of efforts.

Forget Queen Victoria or Queen Elizabeth, Mother Pascal, despite her leg being in irons, would come into the classroom in her black veiled nun's habit with unmatched dignity. She was small of stature and would sit on a chair at a desk, raised up by a mini platform. From there she could see us all, and would warn us of the wicked world. She repeatedly said that if we dressed in sleeveless blouses, or watched the *Johnny O'Keefe Show*, we'd end up with many husbands like Elizabeth Taylor and other Hollywood stars – which seemed utterly horrifying even if we had never heard of Elizabeth Taylor. She said, staring at us, 'I hope none of you is watching the *Johnny O'Keefe Show*', referring clearly to its lurid songs and dancing the twist which everyone knew, in 1963, was on Friday night at 7 pm.

We were too young to be interested, but she interrogated us personally with her searching eyes, which induced us to avoid this show like the plague, even if we didn't really like it and preferred Bugs Bunny and Superman instead. But who needed Johnny O'Keefe anyway, when we had Mother Pascal who probably was on first name terms with the Pope? Poor Buddy Holly and Elvis Presley – we did not know of them either and similarly had no idea that the Beatles were a rising attraction, as were the local Little Pattie and the Joy Boys down the road at Maroubra Beach. While Little Pattie was Australia's answer to the American Beach Boys, I was blithely unaware of it all. In time we got to know their names but Mother Pascal had so imbued us with a suspicion of worldly pop stars that we would have pitied them, deprived as they were, like many others, in not knowing Mother Pascal and her vividly ordered world.

Imbibing the verities

There were other verities we imbibed during that era, one of which was never to walk near an Oleander tree as, if we touched it, death by poisoning would follow. We fervently believed this, so we avoided them. Buffalo grass was somehow connected with buffaloes but we did not know how. Peanut butter was full of vitamins, Sao biscuits were good for you as were Corn Flakes. We knew if we swallowed chewing gum it would stick to the insides of our stomachs and cause long term problems. Spinach would make us as strong as Popeye and bread crusts would make our hair curly. We were told Castor Oil was good for you but never knew why as it tasted so horrible.

My classmates became irrefutable sources of information about life. As I opened up and talked more, many of my sentences began with, 'A girlnaur class said' ('A girl in our class said') which was simply a way of transmitting news of great importance to the world, news which simply had to be listened to. I transmitted long news bulletins to each of my parents always beginning, 'A girlnaur class said' and wondered why they chuckled away.

If we broke a class rule or spoke too much, we would get a whack with a ruler on the palms of our hands. Remember these were the 'olden days'. This was fairly common practice at the time, whether in government or Catholic schools. Insider knowledge at the school dictated that you had to lick you palm several times as you lined up, and the whack would hurt less. In fact, I cannot fathom how Mother Pascal, who was herself disabled, with a leg in irons, could exert any strength to whack anything, so I think it was pretty much a symbolic gesture and an attempt to teach us the consequences of our actions. I was whacked a few times but I cannot remember any pain, but then, I likely attributed this to the furious licking of my hand beforehand. A friend recalls a boy in primary school, who was about to be whacked, grabbing the cane out of the teacher's hand, running off with it, out of the school, and returning with it in several pieces hours later. Then he disappeared from the school for several weeks but did eventually return and resume his education.

We played on swings, slippery dips and had metal monkey bars in our playground, but nothing matched the wooden merry-go-rounds in some parks on which we could swing so fast that we probably escaped mortal injury several times. We did injure ourselves running and playing in the schoolyard and the nuns exhorted us to endure the scrapes and cuts with stoicism. The typical games of the times included 'What's the time Mr Wolf?' with the 'wolf' answering 'One o'clock'; and again, 'What's the time Mr Wolf?', and the 'wolf' answering 'Two o'clock', and so on, until he suddenly yelled 'Dinner time!' and chased us squealing children away.

A friend Lee Kendrick recalls that in her primary school years at St Joseph's Rockdale in Sydney, the boys had a way of holding each other around the shoulders and calling out, over and over, 'Who wants to play-ay, cowboys and in-juns?' Cowboys were still very much alive. Other boys would join them one by one, and also put their arms around their shoulders thus forming an ever longer line, readying for battle, like something from the movie Zulu. At some point the line would be so long that it would be 'game on' with the boys suddenly separating and playing 'Cowboys and Indians'. They chased each other around the playground until some cowboys 'killed' other cowboys and Indians and bodies were strewn over the playground in the massacre on a peace-loving Catholic school ground. In the end it was basically 'chasings' that they played – the staple of children's fun in all ages whatever form it took.

Another standard feature of any primary school was that, for whatever reason, students would sometimes get sick and vomit. When it happened at St Brigid's it would occasion immediate demands by the nuns for help from students. We heard nuns exclaim 'Quick Wanda, get Mary to the basin!' Here again I distinguished myself as an extraordinary 'useless article', as I could not stand the whole scene and would begin to vomit too so that two people then needed help. In another reasonably frequent situation, some students had, to put it bluntly, boils on their bums. This led to respectful if distant sympathy with the afflicted student sitting on half the chair. We almost admired such students with boils on their bums as the seating arrangement looked 'different' and fun.

Of childhood illnesses, some got asthma (not as many as do now), some had their tonsils and adenoids removed, which was exciting as you would get ice-cream in hospital! I was totally unsuited to be a doctor or nurse, as my father told me I was too 'squeamish' – another big word I could add to my list, and so impress Mother Pascal in my early rambles. She might use the word 'galoote' and call me a 'useless article', but I could proudly say 'I'm squeamish but not a flibberyjibbet' back at her with a certain sort of linguistic aplomb.

7

CATHOLICS AND THE WORLD

Onwards we went, into the serious depths of our Catholic education. At St Brigid's we were told we were on the path to become mature Christians – at age 10! For a significant ceremony was looming, the Sacrament of Confirmation. We were prepared in painstaking detail to become 'mature' Catholics and encouraged to choose our special saint to help us along. We sat in class with many pictures of saints before us on the tables, St Theresa of the Child Jesus, St Anne, St Maria Goretti, Saint Lucy among many others. However, as soon as I heard the story of Saint Agnes facing the lions in the arena in Rome, and heard of how her hair grew long miraculously to cover her nakedness, I felt an unaccountable pull to choose her, so I did. My Aunty Zenia was to be my sponsor.

During the Confirmation ceremony we were to face the visiting bishop who would confirm us placing oil on us and was to lightly tap on us the face as a sign of our new strength. We all said, 'The bishop is going to slap us on the face', but we knew that it was really a symbolic tap. But if need be, we were to die for our faith. If we had been told to go liberate Jerusalem from the Saracens in a Crusade, many of us would have given it serious consideration. But no thought of battles or persecution crossed our minds as Australia seemed so far from all that.

It was the early 1960s and the European revolt against all institutions, in particular its Christian roots, was taking shape; but we did not know it and in any case it was 'way over there'. Meanwhile, the Second Vatican Council was underway in Rome, with the triumphalist long line of cardinals and bishops beamed around the world as we sang traditional hymns at Mass.

Not only were we aware of the eternal present, but there was also a concomitant sense that the Catholics were rising in the world, perhaps even gradually taking on the entire world, in the sense of future world domination – at least that's how it seemed in 1962 and 1963![22] While there was still some sense of a Catholic ghetto, there was more a sense of the Catholic ghetto having arrived. We could sing 'We Stand for God and for His Glory' with much confidence, as we expected Catholics to succeed in every area of life, revelling in stories of Catholics who had done well in some sphere and thinking, 'See, we can do it too'.

Most impressive was the fact that America had a President who was Catholic, John Kennedy, and I recall the sense of communal pride among us that this was so. In fifth class, in 1962, some of us at St Brigid's collected newspaper pictures of John Kennedy and distinctly remember showing pictures to another student in my class, Elizabeth Collins, and others who were swept up in the Kennedy enthusiasm. President-Kennedy-Picture-Sharing was a very serious activity for us. This was not just the Church-Militant, this was the Church Totally Triumphant.

Such pictures of President Kennedy became as precious as blotting paper. I kept my newspaper photos in a small cardboard box and we all gazed at the happy Kennedy family as an image of how things should be. In particular, I had one showing the president kneeling in prayer in a Catholic church, which we thought was apt for all presidents, and for anyone in the world. We gazed in awe at Jackie Kennedy and wept when she had a miscarriage, losing their child Patrick. We were all so deeply involved. Surely all the world could see that if a President could be Catholic, then the whole world could follow his example? (Of course we knew nothing of Marilyn Monroe nor of John Kennedy's wayward private life).

 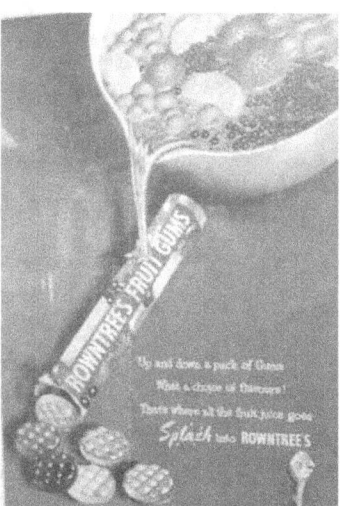

Typical food for 'playtime' in schools in the 1960s: fresh bread with peanut butter and on rarer occasions, like sports days, fresh bread with hundreds and thousands sprinkled all over. If you served this at a school now you might get arrested, with the prevalence of allergies to nuts and the war on sugar. We ate these in copious amounts and stayed skinny.
Right: Rowntrees sold popular fruit gums in that era.

Typical money of the era, some pennies and halfpennies. It cost me three pennies to ride on a bus and nine pennies for an adult in the 1960s.

Typical lollies of the era which we bought by the penny. Musk sticks and raspberries were popular at all schools. We learned how to do maths at the school Tuck Shop by seeing how much our pennies could buy. One penny could buy you one musk stick, or three raspberries, or two mint leaves or, the best value by far, eight chocolate bullets for one penny!

Fantales were only for very special occasions and sold this iconic box while PK chewing gum was sold in small pellets and tasted 'hot', but you never chewed it at school.

Like many other baby boomers, I could remember where I was when I first heard of President Kennedy's assassination on 22 November 1963. I was in the top story of a double-decker green bus in Oxford Street, reading a news headline screaming out from its metal grille on the street, 'Kennedy Assassinated', and was told soon enough that this meant 'killed'. It was such a deep shock that the fifth class President-Kennedy-Picture-Sharing group could hardly speak about it. The idyllic dream of a Catholic President was incomprehensibly gone. This was not meant to happen. We just mindlessly flipped through our pictures, hanging on to a world that had disappeared.

But as with most tragedies, eventually it blended into the sadnesses of life, of things that had faded from the earth, a lost Camelot, things that would never be. We collected pictures of the funeral and of John Kennedy's wife and children, Caroline and John, standing near their father's coffin. But it was not the same – collecting pictures of a funeral could not generate the same interest. Inevitably, the boxes of pictures were stored away somewhere, never to be looked at again. The notion of the world as a 'vale of tears', words we often said in the *Salve Regina*, sank deeper into our souls as I pondered the horror of the events.

Swimming, musk sticks, furlongs and 60s memorabilia

Amidst the tragic world events, spiritual tasks, literary efforts and mathematical problems there was still a lot of fun. We St Brigid's girls would go two by two down the street to the Ladies' Baths in Coogee, to our swimming sessions there. We had our 'tie around the neck' one piece swimming costumes with frills around the hips. Children at school in Coogee were fortunate in having access to this pool, which was protected and isolated from the general beach area. It was not the better known Wylie's Baths but the rock pool known as McIver's or the Ladies' Baths that we visited. We were told that even the nuns went swimming there though this was a strange notion for us as we thought nuns were some kind of angelic beings who did not need to swim.

As well as swimming in this large rock pool at Coogee, which sparkled in the mellow, golden sunlight, this was also the era of Sports' Days with three-legged races, sack races, egg and spoon races, while feasting on pies, sausage rolls and sandwiches covered with hundreds and thousands. In retrospect, it all seems like an ominous scene from a Peter Weir movie with mysterious music playing in the background as the children's laughter filled the green-grassed, white-fenced Coogee Oval. But, even if cultural changes loomed, we were totally carefree. We played with the nearby rhythmical hush of rolling waves as our constant background music. We gazed across the beach and out to sea and thought that China was on the other side of the water, beyond the horizon, and dreamed of exotic journeys there. The aroma of fish and chips shops would occasionally waft through the air and especially enticing was the sense that summer was always just around the corner – perennial summer with its relaxed ambience, flip-flop thongs, languid breezes, sounds of trucks playing 'Greensleeves', visiting circuses and watermelon.

It was still the era also of older English measurements of money and distance. I'm sure our brains were permanently affected by doing calculations such as subtracting £2.17.6 from £8.12.3, or having to multiply or divide them. Halfpennies still existed but not farthings, though we knew what they were. Everyone knew in 1962 that a child's fare on a bus was 3d and an adult's was 9d, for reasonable distances. We knew what fathoms, gallons and quarts were. We knew that 5,280 feet made a mile and that translated into 1,760 yards. We knew what furlongs were and that guineas were a way of saying 'one pound and one shilling' and so on. The future date of 14 February 1966, when Australia changed to decimal currency was still a long way off.

We accelerated our mathematical learning by calculating how many lollies we could buy for our spare pennies. You see, it was high finance to work out which were better, bullets, mint leaves, cobbers, musk sticks, black (only black!) licorice and red gum raspberries for threepence or, if luckier, sixpence. Calculations were made on a daily basis, as we stared at our pennies, waiting in line for the tuckshop lady to serve us. We counted the lollies like bankers operating a New York currency exchange, as the lollies were transferred from large glass jars into little white bags. We knew whether green flavoured ice blocks were better than red flavoured ones, and which paddle pops were best – just ask any Baby Boomer. We had milk delivered to school in half bottles and bought flavoured straws, like scientists seeking to reduce the sour taste, as the milk had often been exposed to the sun for some time. But we still had to drink it. These were the events of our days beneath the canopy of eternity.

Of all the quaint memories I have of that time, there is one that stands out. It was that school rule peculiar to Saint Brigid's, Coogee, and it went like this: if you passed by the nuns' tea room at play time, and saw a hand dangling out the raised window holding a teapot, you were to take the teapot and empty it into the drain below and hand it back to the disembodied hand which then disappeared inside the window – strange but true. Perhaps these pages will be the only ones to record it. This rule was as settled as any Pythagorean law, a reflection of the order of the universe, just as were prayers before lunch, after lunch, the Angelus and sometimes, the rosary –and dangling hands outside windows. Likewise were the compulsory greetings to any nun entering a classroom: 'Good morning Mother Pascal and God bless shoo', upon which she would say 'I am not a shoe girls', making us enunciate 'God bless *you*'.

In the pre-smoking-ban era, children were sold sweets in the shape of cigarettes and would pretend to smoke. The unfortunate name of these packets of 'Fags' was changed to 'Fads' and then disappeared altogether while anyone from the 1950s and 60s can recognise the Arnott's biscuit tin cover, now a collector's item

8

SILENCE, THE *PENNY CATECHISM* AND ATTEMPTS TO GAIN WISDOM

Above all, the pivot of our consciousness in all this remained the Romanesque church of St Brigid's next door to the school. Whether a church was big or small, Spanish Mission style, neo Gothic, modern or Romanesque, I knew it was the One God we worshipped in whatever Catholic church I entered. Somehow, God just stayed there day after day, even when we were doing our parsing, buying lollies or writing – and we personally owned it! The nuns and Coogee parish priest, Father Dando, soon inducted us into a world where the spiritual realities enveloped us ever more deeply. We were encouraged to drop in to the church often for 'visits' and Latin was a language we were to pick up seriously henceforth.

At appointed times, we walked to Masses two by two into St Brigid's church on a regular basis. We stayed so silent that if anyone had a sudden lapse and dared to whisper, a nun's glare obliterated that thought forever. It was not the silence *per se* that was the issue, it was the awareness of Christ's presence in the tabernacle that we were not allowed to forget for even an instant. For the nuns themselves showed us this sacred reality in their demeanour. We were to show respect and to speak only from our souls with the best Person in the world, our Saviour. In the end, learning to remain silent increased our sense of 'otherness' of God, as Father Ranieri Cantalamessa, recent Papal preacher, put it:

> ... the idea of separation, of difference. God is holy because he is completely other with respect to what human beings

can think, say, or do. He is the Absolute in the etymological sense of ab-solutus, separate from everything else and apart. He is the Transcendent One in the sense that he is above all our categories.[23]

This is no post-modern sense of 'différance' or vague piety, but a clear understanding of the abyss between the Creator and the creature. We could not have known who Fr Cantalamessa was but we sensed the message he conveyed in this passage. We could be silent and pray, we could be silent and bored, we could be silent in a world where mobile phones, laptops and iPods were not even on the horizon. We could be silent, and in being silent we were bequeathed a great gift, denied to so many children in more recent times, who hear continual commotion, who are victims of digital noise or who regard the church as a hall. For our part, that silence allowed us to grow interiorly, as if we were monks on Mount Athos, and to reflect on many things, to allow our souls to unfurl, and to listen to the voice within. In fact before we ever heard the term 'Universal call to Holiness' in *Lumen Gentium* (one of the documents of Vatican II), we already were living such a universal call. For the local parish church school was like a convent or monastery in which we sensed that we were 'in the world but not of the world'. We understood Augustine's vision of the City of God and the City of Man, even before we knew who Augustine was. My friend Gail remembers of this atmosphere:

> There are plenty of incidents I remember from my school years that demonstrate the Catholicism of those days. At St Joseph's, Corinda, in Brisbane (I was there for my first two years at school), we stopped work at our desks every half hour to say a little ejaculation [short prayer] such as 'O Sacred Heart of Jesus, I place my trust in you'. All through my primary years, at St Joseph's and at St Finbarr's in Ashgrove, we crowned a statue of Our Lady

in the classroom each May. Every classroom in those days had a beautiful 'altar' with statue and flowers and every classroom had a large holy picture on the wall and nuns dressed in habits. At St Michael's College, Ashgrove, for secondary school, we had a Holy Hour in the chapel every first Thursday, school rosary in the hall before lunch each day and every year a three day retreat with a visiting priest.

While my classroom did not have an altar as Gail describes here, being imbued with the sense of living in the presence of God, bred a receptivity to the spiritual world. We became accustomed to hearing words such as 'transubstantiation', 'consubstantial' and 'spiritual Communion' as the parameters of our existence. We knew parts of the *Penny Catechism* from memory even if we did not understand all its nuances, as we knew that time would fill in the details, the outlines of which we had no doubts. We recited prayers to start the day, prayers before lunch, after lunch and of course the Angelus, kneeling like stately little knights at the words, 'And the word was made flesh and dwelt amongst us', not realising these were the words of the Crusaders on their way from Europe to rescue the Holy Land from the Saracens in the eleventh century, but ready to do battle at Mother Pascal's command.

The world of Catechisms

In reflecting on that 1960s world, it would be remiss not to say a little about catechisms. These were foundations of our lives, just as were God, the angels and the Communion of Saints. They were a brief, concise outline of the teachings of the Church in 'question and answer' form and most Catholics are familiar with them. They have an interesting history and there have been many of them over the years.

I was surprised as an adult to learn that the *Penny Catechism*, so familiar to students of early- to mid-twentieth century, had not existed for all eternity, and was not the only catechism in the world. In fact, St Peter Canisius was one of the first to provide a major catechetical text for Catholics in Latin in 1555, in the wake of the Reformation. It appeared in German the following year. This work, the *Summa doctrinae christianae, per quaestiones tradita et in usum christianae pueritiae nunc primunt edita,* began with 211 questions, but by the Cologne edition (1566) this had grown to 222, with about 2,000 biblical citations and 1,200 references to the Fathers of the Church.[24] This was clearly a book to study. While the questions were short, they would banish confusion, some of the answers running to two or three pages. Then there was the small catechism, *Doctrina Christiana breve* (1597), of Saint Bellarmine, used by Jesuits, Benedictines and some orders of nuns. Another catechism was produced by Henry Turberville (d.1677) who in 1649 printed his *Abridgement of Christian Doctrine* at Douay which underwent several abridgements and became known as the *Douay Catechism.*

There were several subsequent catechisms, one being the *Baltimore Catechism.* Yet another was the 'Green Catechism' which was otherwise known as the *Maynooth Catechism.* This was a modified version of a catechism drawn up in 1775 by Dr James Butler, Archbishop of Cashel. In the twentieth century in Irish schools it was known as the *Green Catechism* from the colour of its cover. But perhaps the one which became best known to the Baby Boomer Catholics in Australia, if not the entire Catholic world, was the *Penny Catechism,* which initially cost one penny, also sometimes called the *Green Catechism* because of its green cover, which was used for religious instruction in Australian Catholic schools during the 1950s and 1960s.

There were 370 questions in the *Penny Catechism.* We could, as a class, chant correct answers to the following questions:

Silence, the *Penny Catechism* and attempts to gsin wisdom

1. Who made you?
God made me.
2. Who is God?
God is the Creator of Heaven and earth and all things.
3. Can we see God?
We cannot see God because He is a spirit without a body.
4. What is God?
God is a Spirit infinitely perfect.
5. Had God a beginning?
God had no beginning. He always has been and He always will be.
6. What is the greatest truth we learn about God?
The greatest truth we learn about God is the Blessed Trinity.

I used to like very much saying the part about 'God had no beginning. He always has been and He always will be'. And question 14 gave us the purpose of our lives.

14. Why did God make us?
God made us to know, love, and serve Him, and to be happy with Him forever in Heaven.

We sincerely believed Mother Pascal or someone would flesh out the details of this statement as time went by but that this was enough for the present. In fact the *Catechism of the Catholic Church* (CCC) published decades later did just so, in a more reflective tone, giving this answer as to why God made us, in the first paragraph:

God, infinitely perfect and blessed in himself, in a plan of sheer goodness freely created man to make him share in his own blessed life. For this reason, at every time and in every place, God draws close to man. He calls man to seek him, to know him, to love him with all his strength.

... when the fullness of time had come, God sent his Son as Redeemer ... In his Son and through him, he invites men to become, in the Holy Spirit, his adopted children and thus heirs to eternal life. (CCC, 1).

But the good old *Penny Catechism* had a strength in stating briefly what life meant and how to live in the here and now. For example it even told us all how to end the day quietly. The final questions of the 370 questions are:

369. How should you finish the day?
I should finish the day by kneeling down and saying my night prayers.
370. After your night prayers what should you do?
After my night prayers I should observe due modesty in going to bed; occupy myself with the thoughts of death; and endeavour to compose myself to rest at the foot of the Cross, and give my last thoughts to my crucified Saviour.[25]

And all this was read by primary aged children! We also learned about offering our sufferings in union with those of Jesus for the conversion of sinners. While this may be weird to non-Catholics, it was not for those of the *Penny Catechism* era who knew that even if they drank their Milo and played chasings before going to bed, there was a spiritual dimension to their lives; there was a Heaven, a Hell and a Purgatory. Despite the *Penny Catechism*'s seeming quaintness, it all made a lot of sense to us and was our entire cosmology. It provided an answer for everything. No doubt educational psychologists might bemoan its difference from Piaget or Kohlbergian stages of moral development, or bemoan its lack of pictures. But through this Catechism, for all that might be said in criticism of it, we saw in some sense, the heights and depths of our Catholic faith, for it communicated that there *was* a transcendent

A surviving milk bar in Darebin, Victoria, most having disappeared from Australia

Another surviving milk bar, from the 1950s-60s era in Sydney, the Olympia in Stanmore, looking somewhat the worse for wear. Many went to such places to purchase an ice cream or a milk shake. They have nearly all disappeared now and doubtless this one will too although some country towns are introducing milk bars as 'exotic' reminders of the past. (Right) Milkshakes were mixed in metal containers like this authentic one from the 1960s.

A surviving advertisement for Vincents headache powders in the Olympia Milk Bar in Stanmore, Sydney. You could buy these powders singly with the powder wrapped in a Vincent paper. Many people ruined their kidneys by taking too many of them.

Other consumables common in the 1960s: Peter Stuyvesant cigarettes for the jet-setters and Bex headache powders for those who preferred them to Vincents or Aspros

Before tea bags you used loose tea. Bushels, Liptons and Kinkara were still familiar tea brands in the 1960s and many have attested to the washing effectiveness of Velvet soap.

These brands have survived but this was their packaging in the 1960s and everyone from this era knew about Paddle Pops. Memoriabilia shops now sell these packets and signs for high prices.

(Right) This was the way people relaxed in the 1960s, by stretching out on a relatively cheap plastic 'banana lounge'. We had one. Those who lived through the 1960s and 70s will remember.

world, filled with mystery and wisdom, and gave the outline of that spiritual world to us. A woman who found the *Penny Catechism* after many years, remarks:

> Reading it again, and recalling those brief and elegant answers, was actually like the experience of Proust when he tasted a madeleine and was spurred to start his great novel. This was the faith, compressed and systematised for a child's comprehension, containing everything you needed to know to stay on the path to heaven, along with stern warnings of what would happen if you turned aside. The difference between mortal and venial sin was quite obvious to someone who had attained the use of reason (aged seven, according to the *Penny Catechism*), as was the difference between presumption and despair, as were also the only two destinations at the end of life on earth: heaven or hell.[26]

While repeating answers in predictable rhythm to questions given by the nuns, we were given some solid grounding for the future, even if our belief in the Church Totally and Utterly Triumphant on Earth Right Now At This Very Moment In Coogee was a tad too optimistic at this stage. The *Penny Catechism* could not predict the cultural anti-Christian upheaval to come. In fact, our experience with 'the world', within a decade, would soon reveal a strange set of cultural forces: a rejection of the metaphysical, a destruction of the Christian cosmology and mockery of Catholicism in social, university and media circles. It would reveal a world in which the obscuring word 'values' pointed to moral relativism, with the political quasi 'virtues' of inclusion, equality and tolerance replacing objective truth. But for those who were to rebel against the Catechism's verities, it gave them, at the very least, something to rebel against, while for those seeking spiritual anchors in future tragedies of life, it gave them something to consider and reflect upon more deeply. There was no miasma of meaninglessness in our lives, no lack of a cultural story, as now surrounds so many children's lives in Western countries, leaving them adrift in relativism and anomie. The 'dictatorship of relativism' was unthinkable at St Brigid's in the 1960s, for reasonable thought and reasonable answers to universal questions constituted the parameters of our lives.

We went regularly to the church to attend Mass in Latin as a group. At the drop of a hat, we could reply to 'Dominus vobiscum' ('The Lord be with you') with 'Et cum spiritu tuo' ('And with your spirit'), and recite the Lord's Prayer in Latin. We were told to fast on Fridays and other times too. We ate fish and chips of Fridays, wrapped in newspaper as this is what Catholics did – and you read the paper too while unwrapping it all. We pored over holy cards and were told it was a good thing to do the Stations of the Cross instead of playing, and so at various times, children could wander over to practise this devotion without leaving the school grounds.

We would also 'pop in' for a visit to Jesus and genuflect before the Blessed Sacrament and passing by the church, were to make the Sign of the Cross, though we sometimes forgot. When in the church as a group, we were not to stir, but occasionally girls fainted and were carried out. This was a typical occupational hazard of being in a crowded church and I am sure children at any school or public event remember it well. I nearly fainted once, saw dark spots before me and dared whisper to my friend Karel, without any nun hearing me, 'I'm going to faint'. Karel, like a real trooper helping a comrade on the front lines, helped me to change my sitting position and somehow the phase passed. There we sat so many times, in headbands, pigtails, bobby socks, gazing at the tabernacle and the sisters, who were Christ's ambassadors on earth, and the Pope's personal friends, looked on while we did the best we could to communicate with Christ, do the right thing and not faint.

Silence, the *Penny Catechism* and attempts to gsin wisdom

Westminster Cathedral in Sydney and the holy angels

St Brigid's, Coogee, never failed to impress me as I entered. Its towers dominated in this seaside suburb where there were fewer migrants, most being of Anglo-Celtic background at that time. The church had its own interesting story though I did not learn of it until much later.

Coogee was established as a parish in 1911 by Cardinal Patrick Francis Moran, Archbishop of Sydney, and had its own priest Fr. Edward McGrath MSC who was appointed as first priest in charge by Provincial Fr. Peter Treand MSC. It was Fr McGrath who was spiritual advisor to Eileen O'Connor with whom he established Our Ladies Nurses for the Poor on 15 April 1913, just around the corner from the school, at 35 Dudley Street, Coogee. These nursing sisters helped the poor throughout Sydney, gaining the admiration of all. I once heard an atheist praise the Brown Nurses, having seen them on the streets of Sydney. Eileen had lived in Coogee, in Neptune Street, after the death of her father, as it was a poorer area than Surry Hills and someone had recommended the nursing sisters to Fr McGrath. This same Fr McGrath ended up on the battlefields of World War I as did his successor Fr. James Gilbert MSC (both winning Military Crosses).[27]

As things transpired, on 30 November 1919, Frs. Gilbert and his successor Fr Perkins negotiated the purchase of the property where St. Brigid's now stands – the price was £8,387. Fr. Gilbert had grand plans having visited London and, impressed by Westminster Cathedral, he asked the architect to reproduce a smaller version of that Cathedral in Sydney. Here was Australian planning on a grand scale indeed. Some may have thought him delusional but his dream came true. St. Brigid's was an important design of architect Albert Edmund Bates and was the biggest project in the career of builder Albert Travis. Despite many thinking an imitation of Westminster Cathedral was impossible to fulfil, it happened.

Fr. Gilbert asked the architect to reproduce a smaller version of Westminster Cathedral in Sydney. ... It's a fine example of the Romanesque (or Byzantine period) revival designs of the late nineteenth and early twentieth century, featuring polychromatic (light and dark bands) brickwork and a curved vaulted ceiling under a traditional cruciform roof. Small arched windows and simple buttresses are another feature. Fr. Gilbert specified that the interior be vast and spacious. Six main pillars on each side support the roof.[28]

The first altar was wooden but Fr Perkins decided to replace it with a marble altar and the pulpit, altar rails and wall surrounds also are made of marble. The firm of Melocco Brothers. carried out the work, bringing marble from Queanbeyan of a rich cream colour, veined with ochre tints. It was fortunate at the time that the Melocco Brothers could utilise the services of Italian POWs who were skilled marble workers. The finished altar was constructed with considerable artistic finesse and memorable for anyone who has ever seen it. Nor was it destroyed in the quasi iconoclastic frenzy to destroy high altars in the post-Vatican II decades to come.

Of course, once there was a church, there was need for a school, and in due course St Brigid's school was opened on 13 May 1923, next to the church in Brook Street, Coogee. The parish priest, mentioned above, Fr J Gilbert, who had had such grand plans for the church, sought a school for the parish, which had been founded in 1911, and he organised and supervised the construction of the first school buildings. The Brigidine Sisters at Randwick agreed to administer the school and from then on, it was the support of bricks and mortar Catholics which contributed to the ongoing existence of the school. In 1945, it also provided high school classes to Intermediate level until 1955.[29]

We students took it for granted. Without knowing an iota of the history of Saint Brigid's in Coogee, the altar, statues and pictures, somehow constituted our world, were our own house and we sensed they would remain forever. The life surrounding the church with its cosmic expanse, through the ever present sodalities, groups and charitable societies, gradually seeped into our consciousnesses – grandeur and religious art can have lasting effects on children's, memories and sensibilities.

This was the era when Catholic children joined the 'Holy Angels Association' and sang in the choir. In being admitted to the 'Holy Angels', I wore a little red cape with an angel medal attached and sang of God and the saints at Masses early in the mornings. We sang 'Blood of my Saviour, Bathe me in thy tide, Wash me with water, flowing from Thy side' without hesitation and 'Godhead here in hiding, whom I do adore, masked by these bare shadows, shape and nothing more'. With a business-like sense of Catholic mission, I could arrive at school early enough, take out my red cape, ascend the organ loft, and sing some Latin hymns with the other Holy Angels who had arrived early for Mass *before* school. I clearly recall the climb up the narrow stairs leading to the organ loft, the mix of mystery, dust, purpose, commitment and joy in wearing the red cape. I wish I still had the red cape and medal, but it somehow got lost in later moves in life.

Years later, when I had the chance to travel to Latvia, after the Soviet empire had 'ended', I met my cousins who had grown up in Soviet controlled countries. One was Inga, about whom I had heard so much as a reffo child in Australia. I was well aware of the fact that she had grown up in Communist Latvia at the same time as I was at St Brigid's. She told me she too wore a little red cape at school. But she sang songs to the great and mighty father Stalin as a young Communist Pioneer for May Day and marched with fervour, as all children had to do, in the long parades, wearing red scarves drawn around the neck as a cape. She was fascinated to hear of the Holy Angels red cape and I was fascinated to hear of the Communist Pioneers red cape. I think she came to like the Holy Angels more than I ever managed to like the Communist Pioneers. After the fall of the Berlin Wall and Latvia's reacquired independence in 1991, she turned to Christianity, in this instance, Russian Orthodoxy, as she had married a Russian, and was very impressed with the icons and Byzantine liturgy, part of the post-Soviet revival of Christian belief.

9

UNANGELIC BEHAVIOUR AND THE PLAGUE

The divisions between Protestants and Catholics, over now, were still somewhat alive in the 1960s. I remember unangelic slanging matches issuing from both sides, occasions when after school the local Coogee Public School children yelled to us from one side of the street: 'Yer a dirty Kafflick! Yer a dirty Kafflick!' and the Kafflicks on the other side of the street yelled 'Yer a filthy Public! Yer a filthy Public!' And variations on this theme. This rhythmical mutual accusation with finger pointing went on for quite a while until everyone got tired, picked up their bags and headed home. I never joined in, merely watching in horror at this sad feature of Australian life unfolded.

There also were occasional 'Yer a dago!' sessions by both the Publics and Kafflicks, directed at the respective 'Dagos' among them, showing the unpleasant human trait of former enemies joining forces, if they can find another enemy in common. I was conscious of being a 'Dago', though a light brown-haired one, so I would quickly leave when things degenerated to this level of slanging and make my way home. The fact is, there were not many 'Dagos' around so it was more a question on picking on someone who seemed near enough to be named as a 'Dago', a popular insult against migrants at the time. However, as far as I experienced it, the battles were primarily verbal and I never witnessed any physical fighting though I am certain it went on in many places.

During playtime, we sometimes sang songs such as 'Oranges and lemons, Say the bells of St Clement's, When will you pay me? Say the bells of Old Bailey' without having any idea what the words meant. This traditional English nursery rhyme and singing game refers to the bells of several churches, all within or close to the City of London, so there was still an Anglified dimension in our play. We obviously did not understand its references to money lenders pursuing debtors nor its chirpy refrain, 'chop', 'chop', doubtless indicating a beheading (perhaps referring to Henry VIII?). In this way I learned the inherited songs that Anglo-Celtic children automatically learned in childhood during previous centuries. Others included, 'Here we go Round the Mulberry Bush', 'Jack and Jill went up the Hill' , 'London Bridge is Falling Down' and 'Ring-a-ring of rosies'. This latter song, I had no idea until later, refers to the 1665 Great Plague of London. 'The rosie' we sang about so cheerfully was the rash that covered those afflicted with the plague, whose smell people attempted to cover up with 'a pocket full of posies.' And the final phrase is a horrifying reminder of what happened to nearly a third of the country's population, for all of us would chant while some would 'fall' down to the ground, 'Ah choo! Ah choo! We all fall down', that is perish in the plague!

We had little idea of the gruesome meaning of this and dozens of other ditties we cheerfully sang over several years in the playground. But then, very soon new songs began to fill Western airwaves. We joined in the hippy song, 'Hey Mr Tambourine man, play a song for me', not knowing that they sang about a drug dealer.

It is important, I have discovered over the years, to understand the meaning of the songs one is singing.

Theatre and athletic prowess in St Brigid's hall

At St Brigid's another of the excitements of life was that we also staged school plays which afforded some release from parsing and continual spelling and writing. In one of the dramatic efforts, my friend Karel, all of ten years old, played the part of an oriental emperor who sang in a firm voice, looking very dignified: 'I am

Unangelic behaviour and the plague

the mighty Hoky Poky Tippy Toptop ... and all disobedience by beheading I will stop stop', making chopping gestures as we stood impressed, and not understanding a thing about the plot. But dressed as the Emperor's faithful subjects, singing along, we made chopping gestures in unison and showed we were ready to behead recalcitrant subjects. This must have seemed very funny to observers, as there were very many pale Celtic skins with freckles beneath the oriental garb. In fact there were so many girls in the class with freckles that I came to wish I had freckles too but could only count a measly three on my arms. My friend Karel, who on her father's side was a descendant of the Peter Lalor of the Eureka Stockades, had many admirable freckles and suffered from any type of sunburn as her skin was so pale. Despite her sufferings, I longed to have freckles, just as she did, as I thought they were so cool. Karel and I had become friends when she arrived as a new student in fifth class and we started talking to each other in the beginnings of a lifelong friendship. We compared the lengths of our socks, played hopscotch, ate cream buns, compared freckles and chased each other. We could sing songs, recite ads, play sport and tell jokes only fifth and sixth class students could understand. Visiting Karel's family in Dundas Street, Coogee, I was introduced to my first cup of milky coffee at age ten, and to the joys of small model animals, particularly horses which Karel collected. We even ran around pretending to be horses, in the way imagination can dominate the worlds of young children, or at least did then. We had lots of fun walking along the sea shore, examining sea anemones, while I still wondered what China was like on the other side of the horizon.

During our compulsory Irish dancing classes at Saint Brigid's we did the Pride of Erin and other well known dances. We were teamed up two by two so the little reffo kid with Polish roots and long plaits, whose forebears fought the Nazis and Soviets, danced with Karel, the descendant of insurgent Peter Lalor, the Irish-Australian rebel who had fought in the Eureka Stockade – there was surely some piquant irony to that. A local Coogee lady, Mrs Thelma King, came to play the piano in the school hall and all of a sudden would break out into 'Alley Cat' and Gershwin favourites, when the Irish dances were over.

Regular events were staged in the St Brigid's school hall to show off our athletic prowess. Whole classes in identical uniforms performed gymnastics where girls would lift or lower arms sequentially in diagonal lines with military precision, and then the pyramid routine to rival the Olympic Games. Girls would rush to the centre of the hall as suddenly Mrs King would play a bass note drum roll to indicate a feat of rare gymnastic stupendousness was about to happen. Mrs King would rise to the occasion providing a roll of bass notes indicating high drama. We waited in rapt anticipation. Selected girls would climb up on each other to make a four storey pyramid, on which would climb a thin girl with shaking legs to show she could stand on top of it all for three seconds, as Mrs King went wild with the bass drum roll, putting all the strength and movement of her arms into it, as the applauding audience cried 'Wow'. Then, after this successful feat, the thin girl with shaking knees would clamber down with relief to the continuing wild applause of the audience. Who needed the Olympic Games when we had gymnastic pyramids at St Brigid's in Coogee?

10

CHOIRS, GYPSIES AND SAINTS

The students at St Brigid's not only sang songs about the bubonic plague in 'Ring a ring of rosies', in the playground, but also sang more demure ones of Irish scenes, ash groves, Scottish braes and pretty English valleys in the choir sessions we had each week. We sang 'The Gypsy Rover' with its refrain of 'Ar dee do ar dee do da day' and imagined we were on a misty hill waiting for the gypsy rover. And we sang the following ditty, which is probably the most vacuous one ever written, with great gusto as if it meant something deep:

> In a lovely little village by the seaside
> All the boys and girls are dancing
> You can see them gently swaying the moonlight
> Singing songs of car-ni-val.
> Tiri bomba, tiri bomba, tiri bomba, they are singing all the day
> Tiri bomba, tiri bomba, tiri bomba all the way.

I tried to imagine what the song was about and all I could think of was some South Sea Islanders in colourful shirts singing 'tiri bomba' out of sheer bliss all day long at the looming car-ni-val – as we pronounced it. But one song especially remains in memory. This was high drama. We sang the following with sincere, tragic demeanour and attempted Scottish accents and warbled along as if we were on the Scottish Highlands.

> Ye banks and braes o bonny doon,
> How can ye sing sae fresh and sae fair,

How can ye chaunt ye little birds
And I sae weary full o care.

Ye break my heart, ye little birds,
That warble on the flowering thorn,
Ye mind me of departed joys,
Departed never to return.

We had the older Scottish spellings of the words in our little songbooks and I remember them to this day. It must have sounded awful in our Aussie accents but perhaps we had some redeeming charm, captive listeners forgiving our youth. We sang for the Eisteddfod in which we won nothing. But I took to singing all these songs in my spare time. It is probably a genetic feature of being descended in part from Latvians as the latter sing many folk songs on various occasions. My mother sang Latvian folk songs about rivers, horses, bees and villages as I was growing up and we sang together as she drove along in her Morris Minor, and of course my father and Babcia sang me Polish folk songs.

When I was about 10, as my father and I travelled on a bus one Saturday to the city, again on the top deck of a green double-decker bus, he asked me what I was singing under my breath so I stood up, unaware of any other listeners, and began to sing 'Ye Banks and Braes O Bonny Doon' out loud to him. I sang with raised voice as if on a stage, not realising, as he told me later, that the entire bus load of people were listening, some with tears glistening in their eyes – perhaps wanting me to stop! I wondered why my father had tears in his eyes at the end of the song. Was it that this insouciant singing of life's sadnesses touched a chord in him for the song is about that – 'Ye mind me of departed joys, departed never to return'. I became affected by it all too as we looked at each other in a kind of mournful understanding; that moment of togetherness in the bus has stayed in my memory. In any case after my performance on the bus, there was a little round of applause from the passengers. Many things transpired on those double-decker buses in the 1960s!

At the same time I was often attending Mass at another church, St Francis' in Paddington, just next door to where my mother and I lived. This was a whole world in itself. I saw the Franciscan priests walking with their knotted ropes at the side indicating the vows of chastity, poverty and obedience. I went with my mother to Mass there, and we knelt side by side, each holding our Missals following the priests' words, deeply immersed in their solemnity. It may as well have been the archangels before us as I remember the pervasive sense of reverence. I recall saying 'Introibo ad altare Dei, ad Deum qui laetificat juventutem meam'. I can still say sections of the Mass from memory through hearing it repeatedly in childhood, whether from Mass in the main body of the church or at the little side altars where parallel Masses were being said. I also see in memory, very vividly, the parish priest Fr Patrick scolding an altar boy rather loudly as he had brought the wrong items to him at the altar at one point. But the altar boys were generally a competent lot, with their capes ('cotta'), cassock and thin legs sticking out from beneath, a permanent fixture of a Catholic culture which looked as if it would never disappear. My mother, who had a deep spiritual sense, ended up becoming a Franciscan Tertiary and I learned to say the 'St Francis prayer' at that time along with her. We followed liturgical feasts and saints' feast days and it seemed impossible to imagine a world without them.

We would ask Saint Joseph to help us, call out to Saint Jude, Hope of the Hopeless, and ponder the life of Saint Bernadette who saw the Virgin Mary at Lourdes and Saint Maria Goretti, who was killed resisting a lustful assailant. Everyone loved St Thérèse of Lisieux and St Francis of Assisi and continually begged St Anthony to find their keys and a parking spot. I did not yet know that St. Joseph of Arimathea was patron of undertakers, morticians, and pallbearers, St Joseph Cupertino was patron of pilots and that Blessed Columba of Rietti was a patron against sorcerers, among the plethora of patron saints that fill the Catholic world.

I also attended the Latvian community Mass at Flemington and the Polish community Mass in Ashfield and heard the songs sung there with such passion and lament by migrants far from their original homelands. There were different saints greatly admired there like St Jadwiga (d.1243) and St Wojtek bishop and martyr (d. 993). I learned years later that the Catholic school at Bathurst, west of Sydney, was named after the Polish saint, St Stanisław Kostka (d. 1568) who died at 18, though I have never been able to find out why.

The litany of saints and would-be saints and martyrs in Eastern Europe were a constant in my childhood. And no wonder, as there were more martyrs in the twentieth century, many from Eastern Europe, China and Africa (and probably most will remain unknown), than in the nineteen preceding centuries. I was regularly hearing stories of living martyrdom like that endured by many Latvian bishops. I heard of Monsignor Julijans Vaivods who was imprisoned by the Soviet authorities from 1958 to 1960 and who struggled to keep Catholicism going under a Communist regime in Latvia. In 1962 he became vicar general of the Metropolitan Archdiocese of Riga and in 1964 was consecrated titular bishop. I heard the names Jāzeps Rancāns and Boļeslavs Sloskāns who were Latvian bishops in exile and struggled to maintain the Catholic identity of deracinated, displaced Latvians outside Latvia. There were pictures on our wall in Paddington of these 'white martyrs' and many like them. The Latvian chaplains in Australia, Jesuits Father Gaidelis and Fr Becs, kept their community informed of the situation in the home country, week by week, and of how Catholic clergy and nuns were bearing the persecution under Soviet rule.

While some Westerners in the 1960s were infatuated with

Marxism, or versions of it, my family had an inbuilt immunity to this as they had experienced it and had family members living under it – no room for illusions there. It was a reality that thousands were dying for their faith where Marxism reigned supreme. When they first heard of him, both my parents well understood Bob Santamaria and the Movement. The effect of Santamaria has been well described elsewhere in books, more recently by Gerard Henderson, Greg Sheridan and James Franklin, but my parents knew no DLP members, no authors, no politicians and never went to meetings. Like many migrants they were cut off from the mainstream of Australian political life.[30] But the notion that Santamaria, a greengrocer's son, started a movement to counter Communist infiltration of the unions, made great sense to them and to people who were suffering from the effects of Communism first hand. They read about Santamaria and sensed that he 'got it'.

What my parents could not understand was why some Australians were attracted to Communism. Why would anyone be attracted to an ideology that persecuted so many, especially those of religious belief, was built on lies and imprisoned millions who dared disagree? They did not know of the leaders of the Frankfurt School, William Reich, Herbert Marcuse and Grigory Lukac, who were introducing cultural Marxism in the U.S. to destabilise Western society. They did not know of Saul Alinksy's revolutionary manuals preaching agitation in the West. My mother happened to have some Communist sympathisers among her patients in Paddington and often heard them attack the rotten capitalist West. But she stayed silent as they fulminated, even though they knew she was a refugee from a country under the Communist yoke. I just remember hearing it and being puzzled too. Like my parents, I could not understand why some were indifferent to Communism's global assault on freedom, and their mass killings of millions. Those from Australia, who did Potemkin village tours of Eastern Europe, believed everything they were dished up. My family were quite astounded and crushed when Potemkin-village-utopian believers were told of the abuse of human rights in Communist countries and still praised the Communists. This allegiance seemed confused for if there were injustices, it seemed to make sense to repair the injustice, but not to destroy entire societies, cultures or kill millions. Against this amoral revolution, the Irish triumphalist approach of standing up for the faith seemed to make eminent sense. There was a war between those who believed in God, and those who wanted to exterminate Christianity from the face of the earth. We were aware of how terrible it would be, if freedom were taken away, as we had family members experiencing that very oppression.

Peripatetic travels around Paddington and TV ads

In the early 1960s, when my mother was well and worked as an assistant doctor, we visited places together on her rounds – poor people, rich people, and characters including Communists! She was known as the 'migrant' doctor who had come from some exotic faraway place that no-one really understood. She worked very hard and her patients loved her. At one stage she was asked to check the general health of nuns in a convent. We went to the Franciscan Missionaries of Mary in Point Piper and not only was I astounded by the nuns' white habits but also by the extraordinary beauty of the convent setting, overlooking Sydney Harbour (the nuns have since sold it). I had never seen anything like it as I gazed in awe at seaplanes taking off in Rose Bay.

From this convent, the nuns helped many poor with food, clothes, medicine and holidays and cared for the aged, They always reached out to help as many poor people as they could, as that is what nuns did, particularly Franciscans. As a child of a 'broken home', even though my mother worked as a doctor, I was left there sometimes during the week, for days at a time, minded by the nuns and so I had almost free rein in the many rooms of the 'retreat house', and often went to the chapel. I hid in laundry baskets sometimes as a game, and walked around the terraced gardens, visited the chapel and then looked at it from above on a mezzanine floor where the retreat house was located. I read about the saints' lives and helped chop carrots in the kitchen. This pretty setting (after the nuns sold this property they moved west) was very different from the two rooms we lived in, in Paddington, and my father's simple rented rooms. In the peaceful chapel, I sang 'O Salutaris Hostia' and 'Tantum Ergo' along with the nuns, as I knew these hymns from memory. I gazed with longing at the devotional gift shop with 'glow in the dark rosaries', saints' pictures, mini statues and edifying books. A nun called Mother Columbkille taught me to play a Christmas carol on the piano and was very kind.

But stays at the convent were brief and usually I saw the poorer, unpainted terrace houses my mother and I visited in Paddington, with their leaking gas and musty odours, and people who often could not pay – no Medicare then! My mother was very soft-hearted and took no money from several patients who expressed their gratitude by giving whatever gift they could to her – chairs, cakes or vases. She also loaned me to some patients so I could do some cleaning and be company to elderly, lonely people and in general to be a 'helper'.

As this was also the era of the beginnings of television, along with the ever present cosmology of angels and saints, I remember we students at St Brigid's at Coogee were introduced to the worldly sphere of shows such as *Lassie, Bonanza, Superman, Ben Casey*, not to mention *The Danny Kaye Show*. Sometimes I even watched the test pattern on TV in the holidays, waiting eagerly for the first programs at midday – news and a midday movie. But we avoided the *The Johnny O'Keefe Show* which Mother Pascal had continually condemned. Mother Pascal was always right.

In the midst of this nascent influence of TV, we children also became very familiar with advertisements. At lunch times, in our black box-pleat uniforms, we would sit on side steps of the school and sing TV ads in their entirety. This was genuine, spontaneous street theatre with dramatic gestures and blood curdling screams. We could say 'Take Vincent's with confidence for quick three way relief', though we had no idea what the three ways of relief were. We sang songs for Silvikrin shampoo, Aeroplane Jelly, Surf washing powder, Ford Pills, Colgate Toothpaste (didn't 'university tests' prove it was the best?) and any other ad that would come to mind. We could remember every single word, which gives one pause for thought as to the effectiveness of brainwashing. Our favourite was the Mortein ad in which volunteers would enact the death of Louis the fly with exaggerated gestures while we all sang: 'One spray and Louis da fly, apple of his ole mother's eye was Louis – poor dead Louis, Louis da fly – a victim of Mortein'.

No operatic heroine, Turandot or Mimi, died with more grandeur and tragic, choking sobs than the primary school children enacting the death of Louis the fly in 1962 on the stone steps at the side of St. Brigid's school in Coogee – and as we sang, an era was dying too.

And on to the end ...

As time was slowly and inevitably drawing us to the end of this age of certainties, interweaving schooldays and spiritual horizons into a unique, potent heritage, we simply lived in the moment and hurtled with insouciance to the next big step in lives, going to high school. Would I ever make it, would this reffo kid ever get to such dizzy heights?

Having learnt about the Mass, the Sacraments, the Bible, the *Penny Catechism*, the Church Militant, the Church Triumphant and the Church Totally Triumphant Right Now in St Brigid's, Coogee, street theatre, Dagos, Publics, Catholics, fountain pens, furlongs, parsing and the Primary Final, I became aware things were serious for we were seeking to ascend the lofty heights of Mount Zion, namely high school. After wondering if I would ever get there, the reality was just around the corner. The days of the Holy Angels and the pride of Erin came to an end imperceptibly and without fanfare, simply fading into a mist. But ineradicably etched on our souls was the transmission of an entire culture, its otherworldly realities more real than many other supposed 'realities' we saw in our daily lives, no matter what their tragedies and moral confusions. Whether one came from a broken home or not, a poor home or rich, Irish, Aussie, Polish, Maori or Chinese, the nuns had succeeded in passing on the essence of Western civilisation in six years – no mean feat!

One of the courtyards at the Brigidine school. Inside the door to the right was my Year 7 class in 1964 which was taught by the very patient Mother De Pazzi, sister of Mother Pascal.

Mother de Pazzi taught for many years at Brigadine and was the sister of Mother Pascal. We annoyed Mother de Pazzi with endless sophist questions about our faith. Despite this she remained very patient with us.

11

BRIGIDINE, BABY BOOMERS AND CROWDED CLASSES

Most school children, whether from state or religious schools, usually remember their first day of high school. Suddenly another set of buildings appeared in our lives – large, impressive and indicative of serious purpose. I went with so many baby boomers to the most appropriate Catholic high school, in my case, Brigidine Convent school in Randwick (now called Brigidine College), which most children at St Brigid's, Coogee, attended. Its solid, cream-coloured buildings rose above houses near the place called 'The Spot' in Randwick and seemed an impressive visual focus in the whole area. It was odd that I attended a school not in my suburb, as I still lived in a small flat in Paddington with my mother, travelled by bus each day, and stayed with my father most weekends in inner Sydney. But I was not the only student who travelled in this way for the school was well located for transport. Brigidine was both a day and boarding school. In the 1960s, an entire upstairs section of the main school building housed the boarders, dormitory style, with a nun watching over them at night. So people came from afar to the boarding school, and travelled from faraway suburbs because they chose this school and were able to be enrolled.

It was not an elite Catholic school, but was a well-known one which generations of the same family might attend because it gave a 'good education', academically and spiritually. This College at Randwick was founded by the Brigidine Sisters in September 1901 and had a Latin motto 'Fortiter et Suaviter' meaning 'With strength and gentleness'. This was where Mother Pascal slept each night and from where she came to teach us at Coogee. Of course its ever-present Irish legacy surrounded us and was recounted to us on many occasions. Being older, we could understand and become even more familiar with the story of Brigidine convent founded by Bishop Daniel Delany in Ireland in 1807, the re-establishment of an earlier order of nuns which went back to one inspired by Saint Brigid in the fifth century. We repeatedly heard how the first Brigidine nuns had sailed for Australia in 1883 and bravely set up schools to educate us all in Coonamble, Cooma, Cowra and beyond in NSW, Victoria, Queensland and Western Australia. In fact they also set up a school in the Archdiocese of Wellington, New Zealand, in 1898, and they were to spread to the United States, Papua New Guinea and South America. The story was not over yet, as we were part of it.

So, one sunny day in February 1964, I walked through the doors of the new school for the first time in my new grey uniform, with a large group of girls, thus becoming a continuing inheritor of this Western legacy, transmitted through many similar religious schools run throughout Australia, the Josephites, Mercy nuns, Ursulines, Dominicans, Jesuits, Marists, Patricians, De la Salle brothers and Good Samaritans among them. My cousin Michael was already at Marcellin College a few streets away in Randwick while my other cousins, Lucy and Anna, whose parents had bought a Holden years ago, attended St Aidan's in Maroubra which had a high school attached to it.

At Catholic schools in the mid-1960s, the church and school seemed to exist in a seamless union, so the students entered often what seemed like a convent or monastery, with Mass attendance a part of its life. Churches were full and latecomers had to stand in aisles. For the first four years of high school, we still had no idea what Vatican II was, even though it was nearly over, nor had

One of the Brigidine buildings with the school motto on it, 'Fortiter et Suaviter' ('With strength and sweetness').

Brigidine nuns in the habits they wore when they taught us in the 1960s.

A view of Brigidine in the 1950s, pretty much the same as in the 1960s. To the right is the old 'Commercial School' where, in one of its classrooms, I heard the songs of the ' Singing Nun' in 1965 as we sang along in dubious French.

The playing and sports area at Brigidine called 'The Cricket Pitch' where we teenagers engaged in all sorts of activities including softball, athletics, relays, running around the pitch, and basketball on courts nearby. I was useless at sport but won the long jump once simply because I had long legs. There is now an aged care home run by the Greek Orthodox Community on this land.

A second year class photo at Brigidine in 1965. This was the era of pony tails. My friend Karel is in the second last row, 9th from the left with two long dark plaits. In the front row, 2nd from the right is Esther Yee who was a boarder from Rabaul in Papua New Guinea. Yours truly was 3rd from the right in the last row.

Two Brigidine students from the 1960s, Francis Ridley (left) and Julianne Golby (right). Francis came from Ungarie in western NSW, which I thought was Hungary. Julianne told me about a place called Nimmitabel which sounded totally exotic to me. I dreamed of visiting the country towns the boarders came from.

Mother Loyola, who taught English at Brigidine and often quoted excerpts from Shakespeare or her favourite poems when talking to students, here stands at Sydney University, having graduated with her M.A. degree focusing on the poetry of Gerald Manley Hopkins.

we heard of the French anti-Western protests, the Frankfurt School, or *Humanae Vitae*. Dissent was not on the radar as far as we knew, and revolutionaries were thought of as mentally deranged. Perhaps Randwick, or even Australia, was slower to adapt. For the revolution was certainly in progress in America and Europe. The early high school years seemed to follow a pre-Vatican II model, though this changed as time went on. For half of high school, we attended Mass in Latin and sang hymns in Latin, studied Latin – the self-contained world of Brigidine contained the universe with all its galaxies.

Suddenly, we were in big classes. Baby boomer era classes numbered 40 or more students; I recall being in a class of 45 one year. The Baby Boomer era defines those born between 1946 and 1966 during the post-war economic boom when there were high rates of marriage, fertility and high levels of immigration. So during the mid-sixties members of this cohort were well and truly hitting schools. There were always assemblies and gatherings, activities in all directions. There were bands, public speaking competitions, sports, plays, choirs, an orchestra and processions. It was easy to fall into thinking the whole world was like this, Catholics from horizon to horizon, always busy doing many things.

There was a weekly General Assembly in the courtyard at Brigidine. This was no ordinary event. but a momentous occasion during which the principal appeared, standing on an elevated balcony called 'The Folly', which jutted out from one of the buildings. She would announce to the entire school what had been accomplished in the past week, what we were to do, and who had been good and who not. This was almost a prefigurement of the Last Judgement. We looked up at the nun/principal standing on the high balcony as if to the Archangel Michael who had descended from celestial spheres to give a report of earthly doings to humanity and to announce what Heaven wanted done henceforth.

Sometimes there were more formal assemblies under cover in

the local picture theatre, the Ritz, which the nuns owned, strange to say, and the entire school would fill it, wall to wall with students and teachers. This was school on a Cecil B. De Mille scale. Again, there were announcements, philosophical observations, student performances as solos, or in choirs and, most important, a recounting of the story of Bishop Delaney and the Brigidine nuns and the massed singing of the song to Saint Brigid. It was expected that all of us, being part of an ongoing tradition and story, would continue to spread the word of God, as they did, in present and future actions. We also had other occasional guest speakers, a memorable one being Sir Edmund Hillary. There was a 'buzz' in the air for the conqueror of Everest had come to Brigidine, symbolising the fact that Catholics were on the ascendant, climbing all kinds of peaks of achievement in present and future.

Most of our teachers were nuns who were confident and had an immense sense of purpose although there was a gradual trickle of lay teachers as we graduated to higher years. At the time, in fact, there was an acute shortage of teachers in both Catholic and government schools because of the expanding numbers of students, especially at secondary level, with blazing headlines announcing that thousands of Canadian or American teachers would be imported to help meet demand. It seemed natural to many of us that planeloads of teachers from overseas would fly over, as Australia seemed the best country in the world.

My school friend Karelyn Curran with whom I giggled, talked and played all through childhood. She passed away in 2018.

12

LATIN AND THE ELIXIR OF LIFE

Life became busy from the first day in high school, with timetables, recitations of rules and regulations. We were shepherded by the nuns into the subjects considered most suitable for us. While there were many subjects at Brigidine, there was a strong emphasis on music and languages. There was also a 'commercial school' within the larger school. Amidst the daily order of the classes and timetables, there was a general impression of continual industry. Everywhere you saw nuns in habits walking along corridors, up stairs, into secret parts of the convent. If a nun addressed you, the exchange was always polite, as if a saint or archangel was taking an interest in your life and soul. All the teachers seemed totally immersed in their work and expected us to be similarly immersed. Sloth was not an option.

Some nuns did stand out as 'characters' and I say this with great affection. One very memorable teacher was the quietly spoken, yet 'she who must be obeyed' Latin teacher, Mother Conleth, who was a constant throughout my high school years as I studied Latin for all six years. She was a marvellously competent teacher and managed to convey to students that Latin was essential to any kind of semi-decent, self-respecting life on earth. With her there was no negotiation, you simply had to climb the mountain of the Lord by learning Latin with continual translations or you would cease to exist as a moral entity in some way.

Our Latin classes had a predictable form, beginning with 'Salve puellae' ('Greetings, girls') and then advancing to the serious business of vocabulary tests and later, checking our homework translations, including passages from Caesar, Livy and others. This was a huge jump for young children but somehow we went with the flow and managed it. The sense of concentration was intense: it was as if we were at a BHP Board Meeting, adjusting an annual report, or rather sitting with General MacArthur planning a cunning military move in the Pacific. We read through several passages from Caesar's *De Bello Gallico* (About the Gallic War) and I repeatedly learned that the Latin phrase, 'His rebus confectis' was a phrase containing the ablative absolute – clearly of eternal significance – and that Caesar or some other military leader had 'laid waste the field', as you would regularly do if you were a Roman soldier, before proceeding to lay waste another field and then another.

Not to do one's Latin translation homework amounted to human perfidy. This would produce abject horror on Mother Conleth's face. It was betrayal and very personal. Mother Conleth would let you know. So, in this way, I was plunged into learning about wars, political struggles, military tactics and abstruse grammatical problems. It is hard to recreate those times on a page, to bring some filaments back. Day after day we twelve- and thirteen-year-old students grappled with the bloodthirstiness and cunning of Roman wars and got inside Caesar's head.

After a year of Latin, it was actually possible to drop this subject and take on another, but Mother Conleth's focus was on creating large Latin classes which continued as long as she was there, in spite of an anti-Latin trend in other schools. Many were persuaded that the 'more decent thing to do' was to continue in Latin. In this way Mother Conleth upheld the Roman Empire in Australia, as an indomitable force of nature, having us learn endless declensions, having us conjugate irregular verbs and in our final year, she had us proficient at reading the most amazing texts. I recall knowing

A Brigidine student, Diane Ray, in blazer and hat which we had to wear on the street. Perish the thought that a girl would take off her hat.

A group of students at a dinner dance in the 1960s. The nuns in the front row, left to right, are Mother Justin and Mother Celestine; 2nd row, left to right, Mother Germaine, Sr. Adrian Small, Mother Conleth (our Latin teacher) and Mother de Pazzi (sister of Mother Pascal).

Some Brigidine boarders relaxing within the school grounds.

The Legion of Mary group at the school in 1969, with Mother Conleth and Father McManus.

Latin and the elixir of life

Cicero's 'Pro Roscio Amerino' almost from memory for my final exams in Sixth Year as they called it then.

While Mother Conleth was happy that Virgil and Livy were on the syllabus, she was not so happy that the poems of Catullus and Ovid were, as their lurid bits were considered unsuitable for Brigidine girls. Once we were required to go to Sydney University for a special talk designed to help high school Latin students. Mother Conleth gestured to us with her hands from time to time, indicating we should not pay attention to this or that section of the talk. I suspect these were about the lurid bits. She may have been small and quiet, but not even Sydney University could challenge her moral force.

In religious classes, or 'Religion' as we called it, which we had daily in the junior years, we were introduced into wider horizons of the spiritual life and deeper problems. We studied Church history, read biblical passages, memorised them, pondered theological issues such as God being one in three persons, the Incarnation, and reflected on the Crucifixion. We pondered on the virtues and how to acquire them. The religion teacher in our first year of high school, Mother de Pazzi, actually the sister of Mother Pascal, and obviously related to the Pope, who clearly had a wide set of connections among the nuns, invited us to ask questions at the end of class.

She must have come to regret this deeply as question time grew into a monster out of all proportion and showed what Vatican bush lawyers we were and what budding Jesuitical minds we had. I distinctly remember, in a room full of open and shut wooden desks, a girl asking, 'If you were going to Mass, and had fasted correctly, but then food stuck in your tooth got loose and you swallowed it, as you were walking up to Holy Communion, could you still go to Holy Communion because you have eaten something and broken the fast?' Not to mention: What if you had bitten your fingernail and swallowed a bit? This used to drive Mother de Pazzi crazy (and other nuns in other schools no doubt), as similar questions came flying one after another during each lesson. I don't know what made us into such irritating sophists but there was a good aspect to it as we were learning to think and ask questions.

These continual questions had a 'mathematical' dimension, described by Edmund Campion in his memories of Catholic life:

> Looking back on the observance of Lent, one is struck by the mathematics of it all. How much food adults might consume on days of fast was minutely calculated ... Yet Lenten precisians were acknowledging responsibility for their own lives and for those self-inflicted failures called sin. Like sin, fasting was personal; it could not be done vicariously.[31]

Just as you needed to know exactly how much to fast, to make sure it extended to three hours (in the 1960s it was so), you also knew that the devotion of the Nine First Fridays meant that you attended Mass for the First Fridays of nine consecutive months. We also knew a rosary decade had 10 Hail Marys and a whole rosary had five decades with one 'Hail Holy Queen' at the end. But questions still arose, such as whether you could you recite half a rosary? If you did eight First Fridays, did you have to go back and start again? What if you only fasted for two hours and 40 minutes before Mass? What if, what if ... it was your personal responsibility to learn the rules and stick by them? In the end, they were not really burdensome, merely an indication of attention to personal piety and proof you could attend to what you were doing. It was the opposite of spiritual attention deficit disorder, for it encouraged a heightened focus.

In 1967, this Year 9 group at Aquinas College, Ringwood, an outer suburb of Melbourne, typified the large numbers of students in Catholic secondary school classes. Michael Gilchrist (right) was one of the first lay teachers in Catholic secondary schools that were still predominantly staffed by religious, in this case the Christian Brothers.

The same boys in the above photo were taught Latin by Michael Gilchrist and here were engaged in projects on Roman history. The desk arrangement was typical of the time.

A statue of St Patrick inside Brigidine College, Randwick.

13

THE SINGING NUN AND SHUNNING THE DECEITS OF THE WORLD

In my second year, 1965, we had a teacher called Mother Giovanni, who livened up our religion class by bringing in a record of the Singing Nun who sang 'Dominique, nique nique' about Saint Dominic in French. A record player was an impressive piece of technological equipment in those days, the cutting edge of modern progress. Most of us were studying French and could understand at least some of it. The Singing Nun was the famed Janine Deckers, the Belgian nun who had several 'hits' singing religious songs in a modern style. Mother Giovanni played these songs on the school's big, unwieldy record player, as we pondered the fact that a nun had made a record, sang well and was popular all around the world. This was a clear Catholic triumph, as we still thought that Catholicism was gradually overtaking the world, despite President Kennedy's assassination and the evil nature of the Communists who thought they were overtaking the world – poor deluded fools! It seemed fitting that a nun should sing a song about well known saint Dominic which became 'Number 1'. This would be the first of many hits, paving way for the ultimate Church Triumphant which was just around the corner. Soon everyone would see!

We were only 12 or 13 and sang along to the music as best we could. While the world was besotted with the Beatles by this time, we could boast that we had the Singing Nun and 'Dominique nique nique'. Deckers also sang another song as the Singing Nun, 'Entre les Etoiles le Seigneur a écrit ton nom' ('God has written your name among the stars'). To this day I can picture us sitting in rows of brown desks each with a shelf underneath and the imaginary view of the stars and somehow floating above and among us, as vivid as Marcel Proust's memory of his Madeleine in *À la recherche du temps perdu*. We were actually 40 students squeezed into an old room in an old building no longer extant, with paint peeling, trying to sing in tempo in semi-mangled French along with the whirring disc on an old, heavy record player. We really did sing sincerely of the stars and paradise, felt so in the moment, and looked to a bright future – after all it was 1965, what could ever go wrong?

We knew little of the future fate of this singing Belgian nun with whom we sang along then. It was so unremittingly tragic, as I found out later, a true fallout from the 1960s. After her highly successful recordings, numerous problems arose in Janine Decker's life and having left the convent, she became a lesbian and ended up tragically committing suicide as she was being hounded for taxes by the Belgian government, arising from her earlier popular recordings. I was so sad to read this decades later, as it contradicted the carefree atmosphere in which we had sung her genuinely well performed songs and the idealistic image we had of her. Things were happening in the 1960s of which we were still unaware.

As we pursued our various subjects, the sense of the rich heritage of Catholicism continued to deepen. We read from a Catechism, read from books of Church history, even if a good deal was based on rote learning. Our futures were being steadily and surely mapped out for us as the years went on. If we were not to become nuns or get married, we were all to help St Vincent de Paul's or similar Catholic organisations when we grew up, whether single or married, as that is what responsible adults did. We all had a 'mission' in the Church. We were to shun the evils of 'fame, power, wealth and beauty' as these were false allures which would never bring happiness. Not only were we to shun such evils, we felt

One of the many sports teams at Brigidine – the tennis team from 1967. I was forbidden, in stern tones, from playing tennis by Mrs Watts, as this would interfere with developing balanced wrist and arm strength for piano playing.

Marching was a regular activity – here are some Brigidine marching girls holding the school banner.

Another Brigidine college, Kilmaire in Melbourne, showing patriotism and pride at the Commonwealth Parade in 1964. Girls carry the banner with the school motto 'Fortiter et Suaviter'.

My friend Robyn Tandy at her Dominican run Sydney school, Santa Sabina, in Strathfield in the 1960s. Robyn was very talented at sport – and everything else. She is second from the left with a trophy.

Nuns were everywhere in the 1960s such as these Dominican nuns with students from Santa Sabina College in Strathfield, Sydney.

Some Santa Sabina girls with a novice. Meeting with novices often inspired other girls to join the same religious order as the novice had joined.

This balcony at Brigidine College, Randwick, was called the 'Folly' and from here announcements would be made at assemblies in the school yard. It is still there.

On feast days, especially Corpus Christi, the entire school would have a procession, and often we would stop at this point and pray before the statue of the Virgin Mary and Jesus.

pity on any poor person who might end up ensnared and enslaved by constant seeking after big houses, flashy cars, Hollywood fame or succumb to the lure of shady politics – though we liked Catholic politicians. It was one thing to have just enough and live modestly, and another to lust after flashy houses and cars. We devoted ourselves to projects illustrating these evils by cutting out pictures of film stars or wealthy bankers with the purpose of showing how they were trapped and that we would not be like them. It seemed natural to do such a project and I recall cutting out endless pictures of big houses, harbours full of boats, sexy models and stockbrokers, all sad indications of a slippery slide to moral ruin as they might induce one to forget God.

This was not incipient marxism, Communism or liberation theology, just natural Catholic scepticism about 'the world'. It was a lesson in the moderations of one's desires, of setting spiritual priorities. We were only young teenagers, but this made a deep impression on me, and implanted scepticism about riches and promoted thought about human behaviour. I believe that this spurning of wealth and fame led many at Brigidine to local 'social justice causes' after they left school.

At Brigidine, help was conceived, at a very practical level, for overseas missions, for it was incontestable that we were required to further the Kingdom of God by helping our fellow school children in the missions overseas, whatever our state in life, whether we were young or old. At our school, this took the form of making toffees and chocolate crackles for a school in Papua New Guinea called the Hohola Mission, located in Port Moresby (which I was fortunate enough to visit in later life).

My toffee making efforts at age twelve, however, were doomed to utter failure, although they were very well-intended. I recall putting sugar and water in a big pot and waiting for it all to boil but somehow I ended up burning the pot and a hole in the floor at home in our rented accommodation in Paddington. My mother, the landlord and other tenants were not impressed as it was a shared kitchen, so my toffee making career died a quick death. I recall my poor mother had to pay to replace the lino I had burned; I had harmed the world, not helped it.

But other students succeeded where I had failed, and local residents along Coogee Bay Road and beyond, not to mention other students, heroically and dutifully filled their mouths with toffees and crackles that had survived the students' preparation methods and paid for this privilege. No doubt local dentists flourished while the school sent money to our sister school in Papua New Guinea.

14

TRUANCY AND SWINISH ESCAPADES

As young Brigidine students we were told always to behave in a mature, sensible way, but the fact remains that on occasion we did not. In my second year of high school, my class was placed in an old building called 'The Commercial School' which was truly old and in fact reaching the point of falling apart – this being where we had sung 'Dominique' along with the singing nun. This section of the school mostly catered for those girls who, in the past, would not have proceeded to the Leaving Certificate but would leave after third year and undertake a secretarial or business course.

Again the Catholic world seemed so self-contained that students could make a smooth transition from this commercial school to Saint Patrick's Business College in the city and no doubt then gain employment with a Catholic firm, thus avoiding possible anti-Catholic prejudice and, more importantly, keep the faith by working in a Catholic atmosphere, and then presumably meet a Catholic, marry a Catholic and raise Catholic children. In the past days of lingering sectarianism, where advertisements sometimes included 'Catholics need not apply', this was a genuine attempt to help one's own.

By the time my baby boomer year came on the scene, there was less need for these commercial school courses as students could simply leave and enrol in them. I remember giving a briefcase to a friend Mary Zammit who left after Fourth Year (Year 10) to become a secretary. In general, however, there was a real push to complete all years of high school, which under the Wyndham Scheme became six years so the populations of schools burgeoned as did the need for classrooms. I belonged to the second year of this scheme, viewed suspiciously by some of the teachers as an innovation that would lead to no good. We heard about the girls who came before us who had completed just five years of high school and had managed perfectly well, being more mature, sensible and likely better than those the Wyndham Scheme might produce.

In any case, the commercial school within the Brigidine convent school was less and less used for its original purpose and was falling apart; but there was a desperate need for classrooms. Our Year 8 (then called second year) had to squeeze into one of the rooms of this building, before the new one was built, and I recall bits of plaster from the ceiling falling onto our desks, sometimes creating great mirth. As 12-year-olds have little sense, we threw the bits of plaster around and then topped off this activity by pushing the desks forward so the students in front would be squashed and hard pressed to breathe. In that alternative universe of teenage humour, carefree moments and lively animal spirits, we considered this to be funny. We disbelieved nuns who said we were at a 'silly age' and acting like 'giggling gerties' – I added 'gerties' to my Irish repertoire of 'galootes' and 'brazen articles'. We certainly did not 'have our wits about us' for a few years as young teenagers but the laughter did some good to the reffo kid hearing about and thinking of Soviet Poland and gulags.

Moving around Sydney and truancy

While school had its moments of such humour, witlessness and hard work, I was regularly moving around, staying with my mother during the week, and on most weekends visiting the various places where my father lived in Sydney. I got to know several areas of Sydney quite well as my father moved from Darlinghurst to Campsie and then to Petersham or, as my grandmother pronounced it, 'Pitter shame'. My weekend visits to them in various boarding houses resulted in our meeting people from different countries of the world who also lived in these places. A Serbian couple ran the house in Petersham and so my Polish speaking grandmother learned to speak Serbian rather than English. I even learnt a few words of Serbian and met Zora, Milka, Mila, Bobo, Jurica and many other interesting people in this lively milieu.

My father, despite the war and experiences of loss, was a man of extraordinary interests and warmth. He had a genial social manner and could talk to anybody on any subject all the while working in an office at the Water Board for whom he did occasional translations from German to English. He had shelves full of books and drew me into the world of pondering many different subjects. The sense of togetherness deepened with a greater understanding of the past experiences of my parents, as far as I could understand. With my father, questions arose about the war, and we thought of our relations in Communist Poland whom we yearned to meet.

My grandmother met other war survivors at the Polish church in Ashfield where she sometimes went to volunteer as a cook. Later she even accidentally met a fellow concentration camp survivor from Ravensbrück. Babcia saw the global war between Marxism and the rest of the world and spoke with fervour about it. She thought that anyone who went 'soft' on Communists, as she thought the Labor Party had done, were loathsome and encouraging a brutal regime. When election time came, she headed with her walking stick to the nearest polling booth and almost whacked a Labor Party individual handing out 'how to vote' leaflets, saying 'Get out of my way you Communist' in loud Polish. The Labor Party person was unharmed as Babcia was quite weak and could not whack a flea.

With my mother I sang nostalgic Latvian songs at St Dominic's in Flemington where the Latvian community attended Mass. Beneath it all, there was a deep sadness for the world 'over there' from which they were inevitably separated, a sense which, as I said previously, always accompanied my teenage years, even if I did laugh at times like a 'giggling gertie'. My mother was a very sensitive person and people spoke of her 'warm heart' but there was a continual transmission of some wordless sorrows beyond words, a togetherness that was *sui generis* in these fractured times. The Latvian Catholics clung together for decades. Their focal point was Sunday Mass and gathering afterwards for rye bread salami sandwiches and coffee with occasional schnapps or vodka. But one by one they died, their children moved away and the Mass is no longer celebrated there in Latvian. Rather, as a sign of the times, there is now regular Mass in Mandarin at St Dominic's. Latvians, both Lutheran and Catholic, also met socially at the Latvian Club in Parnell Street, Strathfield, in the post-war decades where I took classes in Latvian language, folk dancing and attended choral concerts.

During these teenage years, I remember taking books from my father's shelf, reading about World War II, the Holocaust, with his speaking – as he briefly did at times – about his wartime experiences. This was a terrifying awakening to the details of the brutality of war. One of his books had photos of piles of bodies at Buchenwald which affected me deeply. This was hell on earth!

On my mother's shelves I saw books of Latvian poetry given to her by friends, poignant and heart-rending in the feelings they expressed. People wrote inscriptions on photographs and in books, knowing they might never meet their friends again. As with most children of post-war migrants, there was a deep sense of protectiveness and wanting to 'make up' for what was missing. Rather than teenage rebellion, there was a genuine respect for their goodness. I yearned to make them happy. I knew my family was different. Along with the bustle and hopes of youth, there were attempts to understand what I could not then understand, and that dark melancholic cloud accompanying all our days, the sense that things could not be repaired. Added to our situation was the continual legacy of a broken family. My mother's developing health problems and her sufferings contributed to this sense of loss, with many trips to hospital and a deep inner aching hope that somehow things might be 'fixed'. But they were not.

Truancy and swinish escapades

Contrary to the ambience of the times, to rebel against parents and authority was totally unthinkable for me for there was much to repair, preserve and uphold. I was drawn in to my parents' universe, and my instinct was as compassionate as a teenager's could be, along with all its nonsensical phases while in the midst of all this the Catholic school surrounded me. No matter what happened, here was a world which seemingly affirmed one's existence, dignity, Catholic identity, and was a rock in a world of change and destruction. It was a world whose strength in the face of the world's troubles, and particularly the Communist assault, was fervent, would never disappear, a place where learning, creativity and hope abounded, here in the Antipodes as much as in Nursia, Chartres, Kildare or Cluny.

During my third year of high school my mother and I moved from the Paddington rented rooms to Randwick to live in an apartment, then called a home unit. I regretted leaving character-filled Paddington, with its daily 'events', pervasive rented rooms, terrace houses and back lanes, but this was timely as my mother put a deposit on a unit, and now had some respite from constant night-work in Paddington. She needed to work less due to ill health but she did work, and she made Greek, Lebanese and Maltese friends and especially migrants who had escaped Communism. She tried to assuage their anxieties and griefs all the while suffering herself. Her patients sensed this, identified with it, and loved her, many migrants and Aussies travelling to Randwick to see her in her one room assigned for her work during her 'well' phases.

We lived near Our Lady's Nurses for the Poor and attended their annual fete days. My mother had an especial soft spot for them and it was one of their sisters who actually came to visit her when she was ill and dying decades later. We lived near my cousin Michael and his parents in Randwick, and Aunt Zenia came to visit often and my mother visited her too. Within 10 kilometres of where we lived you could find various religious orders apart from the Brigidines:

the Little Sisters of the Poor in Randwick, the Missionaries of the Sacred Heart in Kensington, the Sisters of Charity in Darlinghurst, the Daughters of Our Lady of the Sacred Heart in Kensington, the Scalabrinians in Mascot, the Franciscans at Waverley. Unbeknownst to us, we had moved to one of the heartlands of Catholic Australia!

As part of moving to Randwick, I was allowed to have a kitten. This enraptured me. I wanted so much to be with this kitten that I could not understand why school should interfere with this.

Now I must publicly confess what I did after so many years. On schooldays, I worked out a way of truanting from Brigidine. Swinish scoundrel that I was, I simply slipped away during a class before lunch, as our new unit in Randwick was not too far away. I would then return at the end of lunch looking nonchalant and rejoin classes. This allowed me to cuddle the kitten I had acquired, play chase the paper ball and no-one ever caught me. As my mother was out during the day at that time, I simply opened our door with my key and let myself in to play with my kitten. I derived such joy from that wonderful Persian kitten. Another means of playing truant occurred in this way. I also would dawdle back from my music lessons and managed to hide myself in the bushy part of the school, most of which does not exist any longer. It was just an overgrown mini forest, I thought, and I lurked inside it having some respite. Perhaps there was a Marvellian desire to seek 'a green thought in a green shade' but I think I just wanted to escape classes for a while. Thankfully this did not last more than a few months, saw the error of my ways and stopped truanting. This is all very darkly ironic as, later in life, for a few years I was a truancy officer for the NSW Department of Education before I became a psychologist. And I must say I enjoyed the job immensely, as I could uncannily read the mind of the truants several steps ahead, to their dismay, and coax them back to school. I was a surprisingly successful truancy officer. If you want to understand the mind of the truant, just ask me.

15

FRIENDS FROM FARAWAY PLACES, MY CAREER AS A SMUGGLER

Part of the passing parade of events at Brigidine, for me, was the litany of Irish names at roll call: Delaney, Doolan, Hanrahan, O'Brien, Quirk and Curran, the latter being the name of my friend Karel, who had come to Brigidine too. But there were others who provided evidence of a strong contingent of what Arthur Calwell called 'New Australians'. There were a few names of Italian, Chinese, Hungarian and Polish background: De Lorenzo, Yee, Gombos and Skowronska. But over and above all this, it was novel for me to hear of the country life of boarders from Bundanoon, Forbes, Parkes, Ungarie and Walgett, very exotic place names for a reffo kid. It may as well have been about Mars or Pluto as these faraway places which I had never seen became imaginary lands, for the reach of the Catholic universe went far and wide.

At the end of term many students would pack and get ready for train trips back to these country towns, no doubt filled with adventure, probably even castles. On their return at the beginning of term, the boarders would always be asked in class, by nuns doing the rolls, questions such as: 'How are the Flanagans at Cooma?' or 'Do you know the Hanrahans of Coonabarabran?' or 'How are the Murphy family getting on at Forbes?' The networks of Irish Catholic connection seemed to spread around all of New South Wales, and no doubt throughout the entire world. I may have known of Berlin and Warsaw, but I longed to see Coonamble and Boggabri.

While Karel and I remained constant friends in school and

beyond, and laughed as teenagers at so many things we thought funny then, we were also exposed to the wider world of the Brigidine universe. One friend I made was a Chinese boarder from Papua New Guinea, Esther Yee, a thoughtful, quiet girl, whose parents ran a business in Rabaul and who told me how much she liked cream cakes. While the nuns fed the boarders very well and they got cakes and fruit after school, these teenagers always seemed to be hungry. Esther asked me to find her some extra cakes, the cream cakes she especially craved. So I entered the world of smuggling, buying them at the 'cake shop down the street' and carrying them to school under my blazer. She was delighted when I gave her the paper bags with long cinnamon buns with extra cream inside.

Esther and I saw each other a few times after leaving school, but then we lost touch. It was only through a chance contact, after 40 years that we met again, through a lady working in a state school who had met me and mentioned my name to her. Now that is an unlikely coincidence but it happened, for Esther, in talking to this friend, remembered she had known a girl called 'Wanda', so after emails and phone calls, we met again after all these years. She was a pharmacist by then and was married with two daughters. Her parents' export business got wiped out after a nearby volcano erupted and destroyed the Papua New Guinea town of Rabaul. Esther moved to Port Moresby and then came to Australia. When we met in Sydney such was the effect of her school memories, that she asked to see the cake shop at 'the Spot' in Randwick that she had liked so much. I took her there and we gazed at it for quite a while, standing on the footpath, lost in memories of those carefree, cake smuggling times.

Another school friend, Francis (sic) Ridley, came to the boarding school at Brigidine in year 11 and had many interesting things to relate about where she came from – Ungarie – which I thought originally was Hungary before she explained it was 'out west near West Wyalong'. Francis was a tall girl, outgoing, with a very engaging smile and I liked to hear her stories. While not having an Irish name, Francis had the name of the famous inventor of Ridley's Stripper, who eased the task of farm workers on wheat fields. That was fame indeed. We had learnt about this in primary school. Mother Pascal was right and now before me was a descendant of the famous inventor. This confirmed the infallibility of the nuns at St Brigid's, Coogee, who had taught us about Ridley's Stripper and MacKay's Harvester. Francis clearly enjoyed the boarding school and had a warm, lively rapport with the nuns as well as with us. I was fortunate to meet her in later life and she shared her memories of coming to Brigidine from faraway Ungarie. Here is part of her story as told to me:

> When I was about 13 or 14 on one of our trips to Sydney, Dad was driving down Parramatta Road and we passed Sydney University. Dad said to me 'That's where you will go one day'. While most farmers considered education wasted on girls Dad was different. He recognised that I worked hard at school and would benefit from higher education. The nearest school that taught to HSC level was West Wyalong High, 35 miles away. Two of my brothers, Quentin and Clarry did the HSC there by boarding with our Uncle Trav and Aunt Nell Ridley who lived six miles out of town. One of my younger sisters, Elizabeth boarded with Dad's cousin Glen Ridley and his wife Janice, in Burcher, a little village 11 miles from home where we often went to Sunday Mass. By then there was a bus to take the local children to high school. Rosemary, my older sister, left school after completing the School Certificate as did Adrian, my other brother, and Lindsay, my youngest sister. Some years later there would be a bus from Ungarie Central to West Wyalong High School. I was the second child and the lucky one because I had the privilege of

attending a boarding school. Dad decided we would go to Sydney and visit some Sydney boarding schools. First we went to Loreto at Normanhurst which was very close to where Dad's sister Clarice Miller lived on Pennant Hills Road. I was about 15 and was wearing high heels and a pretty dress thinking I looked very grown up. The head sister explained to Dad that there were no vacancies. But Dad and I went away thinking she thought we weren't good enough. We had better luck with the Brigidines at Randwick where Mother, whose name I don't recall, told Dad they would take me.

During 4th Form at Ungarie Central School I sat for the Commonwealth Scholarship exam and the State Bursary. I missed out on the scholarship but gained the Bursary. Unfortunately the Bursary was means tested and Dad's income for the year on which the Bursary was assessed was just a little too high. If it had been the year before or the year after we would have qualified. We thought it unfair that no account was taken of the fluctuations in farm income due to seasonal factors such as drought, hail damage or frost damage to crops, low prices for wool and wheat and so on. My darling, generous mother came to the rescue and used the money she had saved over the years from the Child Endowment for all of us seven children, to pay the school fees.

So I began the last two years of high school as a boarder at the Brigidine Convent, Coogee Bay Road, Randwick. When Dad dropped me off on my first day in January. 1968 and walked away, I felt utterly alone. It was early and there were only two girls from the fourth form there. I walked around with them as they chatted about their holidays but I felt like an outsider. I started to feel better when the new fifth form boarders began to arrive and I met some of them, Mary Mullins and Dianne Ray from Forbes and Julianne Golby from Nimmitabel near Cooma.

My goal was to get a good education and then go to university. This time the Commonwealth Scholarship was awarded on the basis of the HSC results and not an exam. My hard work at school paid off and I was awarded a scholarship. I will never forget the day in January 1970 that the Commonwealth Scholarship results were printed in the *Sydney Morning Herald*. Dad drove to West Wyalong to get the paper and as I anxiously perused it what a thrill of delight and relief flooded over me when I saw the results and the prized Commonwealth Scholarship. My going to University depended on that as Dad had said he would not sign the bond even if I won a Teacher's Scholarship, which I did. But I received so much more than that in those two years and I count those days as a truly great blessing thanks to the Brigidine Sisters.

These days it is politically correct to harshly criticise members of religious orders and blame them for all kinds of personality damage and to lament any time one may have spent under their care. However I am deeply indebted to the Sisters and am writing these words to pay tribute to them for their generous and selfless service to God and their neighbour.

Most students I met in later life, like Francis, looked back on the years at Brigidine with quiet awe and gratitude. This Catholic school had provided a still point in a turning world, whatever the insecurities and problems of our parents, whether we were rich or poor, orphaned or from large families, we belonged in this convent school and to the magnificent cultural/spiritual world transmitted by the nuns. It may not have been everyone's experience, but it was ours. It may have been a disappearing world, but not for us!

Note the inkwells on these typical desks of the 1940s, 50s and 60s. They gradually disappeared and no doubt are now collectors' items.

16

THE LURE OF LITERATURE AND LANGUAGE

While others grew in mathematical prowess, I plodded with equations though I liked algebra. Rather, I had always had an inclination for using words and hence was drawn to literature, so my memories revolve a lot around these classes. After Mother Pascal's encouragement of our efforts in primary school with inkwells and fountain pens, I was inexorably drawn into the world of poetry and prose. I recall learning many lines from memory, as we still did in the 1960s, a weird historical detail in itself. For example, we recited 'A Shropshire Lad' by A.E. Housman:

> Loveliest of trees, the cherry now
> Is hung with bloom along the bough,
> And stands about the woodland ride
> Wearing white for Eastertide.
>
> Now, of my threescore years and ten,
> Twenty will not come again,
> And take from seventy springs a score,
> It only leaves me fifty more.
>
> And since to look at things in bloom
> Fifty springs are little room,
> About the woodlands I will go
> To see the cherry hung with snow

It must have seemed funny for 13-year-olds to say with solemnity 'Of my threescore years and ten, twenty will not come again' but we did, as if we 20-year-olds, facing imminent death. We also recited triumphal poetry from the colonial era and I especially remember John Masefield's 'Cargoes' which we chanted out loud in class as if we were all mini Rudyard Kiplings:

> Quinquireme of Nineveh from distant Ophir,
> Rowing home to haven in sunny Palestine,
> With a cargo of ivory,
> And apes and peacocks,
> Sandalwood, cedarwood, and sweet white wine.

And so on. The horror of having animals as cargo escaped us then, though I did wonder about it. But I chanted the entire poem in rhythm, along with the rest of the class, imagining exotic places – and can recite it from memory to this day. While other students were immersed in mathematical problems and were very good at them, I was being swept away by the world of the imagination presented in literature. We memorised Shakespearean passages, e.g., 'The quality of mercy is not strained' and pondered Hamlet's problems as if they were our own. We deeply reflected on Shylock's situation in *The Merchant of Venice* and had inspiring teachers of English who gave us a true mastery of the language.

One teacher of English I remember in particular was Mother Loyola who read poetry in class and inveigled us all into believing literature was the key to understanding humanity and therefore we should treat it with utmost seriousness. So along with Latin being the elixir of life, here was literature too. It was an initiation as if to an arcane society, not a Dead Poets' Society exactly, as we felt they were all very much alive. Mother Loyola had an enormous influence on many students as evidenced by the packed church at her funeral years later including crowds of former students, myself among them. Many have attributed their love of literature to her. She led us along the paths of Western civilisation and its literary treasures, up and down poetic dale and up into the clouds. We were immersed in the poetry of Gerard Manley Hopkins since Mother Loyola, as I later learned, had completed a Masters' thesis on his work and clearly loved every line and word of his writings, saying them slowly, savouring every phrase. We heard her read 'The Kingfisher' with rapt immersion in the images evoked, gazing into some distant scene which only she could see. Here are lines from this poem to convey something of her predeliction and passion for this kind of poetry. Imagine a voice here, full of quiet drama and intensity, reciting this slowly:

> As kingfishers catch fire, dragonflies draw flame;
> As tumbled over rim in roundy wells
> Stones ring; like each tucked string tells, each hung bell's
> Bow swung finds tongue to fling out broad its name;
> Each mortal thing does one thing and the same:
> Deals out that being indoors each one dwells;
> Selves – goes itself; myself it speaks and spells,
> Crying What I do is me: for that I came.
> I say more: the just man justices;
> Keeps grace: thát keeps all his goings graces;
> Acts in God's eye what in God's eye he is –
> Chríst – for Christ plays in ten thousand places,
> Lovely in limbs, and lovely in eyes not his
> To the Father through the features of men's faces.

I can't say I understood all this at the time, but I was impressed, even daunted, by G.H. Hopkins' idiosyncratic use of language, having some inkling that he was on to something. I liked the music of his poems, the images that jumped out of the page and sensed that he was in touch with a deep spiritual reality embedded within the natural world. The world was never just what we saw, it was a highly mysterious, rich interwoven tapestry of a thousand hidden things and it was our duty, if we reflected on it, to uncover those myriad things. I became accustomed to using words like 'beauty' and 'truth' with all the infallibility and dreaminess of teenage mysticism and to see the world through the eyes of Shelley and Keats, at least their poetry, if not their lifestyles.

Mother Loyola laced her comments to us with quotations from the Bible, poetry or Shakespeare, so such language became familiar to us. You heard a quote often enough and you remembered it and you were likely to receive literary answers to the most simple of questions. When speaking of the future she might say with Shakespearean solemnity, 'There's a divinity that shapes our ends, rough hew them how we will', even if you were talking about an event next Tuesday. She might quote Wordsworth in referring to the misuse of time saying, 'Getting and spending we lay waste our lives'. She might quote from the Psalms saying 'deep calls to deep' or 'In your light we see light' and stare ahead as if she saw something so mysterious in the cosmos that we strained to see also. She was a very poetic, widely read, spiritual person, perhaps a mystic. She also spoke in a soft voice and this was a very cunning teaching technique. While not raising her voice, the look that accompanied the soft voice could be that of a quiet assassin, expressing displeasure. Still she was no assassin, in the end being a real softie who could quell a philistine, unruly class simply with her 'presence' and a glance. I tried the same thing once in later years with an unruly class I taught but it didn't work.

By this time, as high school wore on, I became, as most of us did, accustomed to the separation of appearance and reality, the ephemeral nature of things, the tragic dimension of life – goodness knows I had seen it in the post-war grief I encountered in my family and friends. Here Mother Loyola showed great kindness to me when she heard of the ill-health of my mother and the latter's spells in hospital and expressed compassion, very meaningful to me at the time. But this sense of the tragic which she was attuned to became part of our maturing in a particular cultural setting. While I procrastinated about Maths homework, I sighed at the passing of time in the poem, 'Margaret are you grieving over Goldengove unleaving.' I knew that Margaret, who could be anyone, in Hopkins' poem was grieving about the ephemeral nature of all things on earth. What did Maths matter when all about us was temporary and passing away. This struck a deep chord with me at age fifteen in 1967 and the poem stays in memory to this day:

> Margaret are you grieving,
> Over Goldengrove unleaving,
> Leaves like the things of man, you
> With your fresh thoughts care for, can you?
> Ah! as the heart grows older
> It will come to such sights colder
> By and by, nor spare a sigh
> Though worlds of wanwood leafmeal lie;
> And yet you will weep and know why.
> Now no matter, child, the name:
> Sorrow's springs áre the same.

I learned such poems from memory. Some might think this poetical behaviour to be somewhat nerdish but if you came under Mother Loyola's influence, you tended to be magnetically drawn into a world of the spirit and imagination and ascended a literary Mount Parnassus like breathing in the air around you. I pondered the fact that Margaret in the poem above, would not care for the 'worlds of wanwood' as one day she would understand the mortal nature of everything on earth. We, who had read the poem, just knew the entire earth is a dying world as all poets from Virgil to Keats had lamented, and that we are all part of this dying world.

This was no small thought for a teenager, but it was part of the spiritual as well as poetic sensibility infused within many of us in this 1960s education. Of course we did not grasp the irony of living through a deconstructing world that indeed was passing away in the 1960s. Our thoughts were more poetical, rather than political.

As well as studying Shakespeare and some nineteenth century poets, we encountered 'The Love Song of J. Alfred Prufrock' which was studied in our final year. Here, in the more 'contemporary' T.S Eliot, was something totally different, not just the pretty words and phrases of 'The Shropshire Lad'. Here we pondered images of aridity and confusion which seemed to match our growing sense of a world which was changing quickly around us with some political dark clouds on the horizon: what did it all mean? Strange winds were starting to weave their way into our lives and questions of who we were and what would become of us. T.S Eliot seemed to me to be speaking of something happening in the world of 1967 but, of course, he was speaking to an entire century. Coming across all this for the first time, in senior studies, there was a deep sense of an ominous, dangerous portent embedded in the lines, some kind of accurate barometer pointing to the approaching seismic shifts going on in the social, political and liturgical worlds around us even as the world continued to trumpet its various forms of progress.

Translating into English for Babcia

While being introduced to the classics of Anglo-Celtic literature and learning Latin and French, I was also involved with language in a more basic sense. I often had to translate for others, notably my grandmother, whose English was not fluent enough to explain what she meant in shops. She once cackled like a chicken to ask for a chicken in a shop which usually displayed them but not on this one particular day. The butcher understood. So, as many migrant children have done throughout the years, I became the

English translator for her in varied situations and even patched up misunderstandings. One of these occurred when I helped in the purchase of sheets. I don't know if was with Babcia or another person but I found myself in a Petersham shop standing near the shopkeeper in a store, with a lady asking, 'this shop haff shits?' An unpleasant situation started brewing. It did not help when the lady said, ever more loudly, 'Shit! Just shit, nothing else', looking around the shop, trying to draw the outlines of some bed linen with her hands in the air. She wanted to buy some bed linen. I understood the need for the long 'e' in 'sheet' and this propelled me to do timely damage control, saying, 'She wants to buy some sheeeeeets for the bed'. All of a sudden the shop-owner realised he was not being insulted and went to the corner where he did, in fact, store some sheets. (These were the days when there were Manchester shops around the suburbs that sold linen and sheets). However, some situations were irretrievable, like the time Babcia bought a 'With Sympathy' card for a young couple on their marriage day and gave it to them. As for any Pole, 'sympatia' is a positive word, and if you express this on some important occasion, as for a wedding, that's good! Imagine when Babcia was told this was a funeral card, *after* she had handed it to the Australian couple, for she did not read the inside greeting, just saw the 'With Sympathy' on the front of it. She never lived that down.

I became accustomed to hearing the accents of various 'New Australians' and even the inventive use of words. I heard some say 'She is suspecting a baby' (she is expecting a baby), 'I have a rupture' (I have a flat tyre) and 'I vont vun letter' (I would like a head of lettuce), not forgetting that I knew no English at all in the migrant camp and must have come out with some clangers as well. But at least I never came out with that greatest English clanger of all time, once written in an HSC History paper: 'Matthew Flinders circumcised Australia with a 12 foot cutter'. Yes, someone wrote that.

Throwing chalk, Madame Meyer Gleaves and the French Revolution

We were educated at a time when French was considered an important global language and anyone with a modicum of linguistic ability was funnelled into the French class. It was a verity in the lingering colonial era that to be civilised meant to speak French fluently. We had a very effective nun for teaching us French in the early secondary years, Mother Lucy, who always had a rather tired and harassed expression as she entered our classes and no doubt we did nothing to assuage it. I think we were restless rats at times but she tried her best to teach us perfect French sounds. She had us take out sixpence, and put it between our teeth so we could get the correct pronunciation of an acute 'e'. So we stretched our lips to the limit and said with distended smiles 'é, é, é'. As well we all seemed to sound like a bunch of magpies, making our 'è grave' sounds, something like, 'eh, eh, eh'.

How we annoyed Mother Lucy as we performed death-defying jaw stretches, particularly on the summer afternoons when we wanted the day to end. I recall we annoyed her so much that she picked up a handful of chalk one day and threw it at the class in frustration. I don't know what we had done but we had that teenage belief that our sense of humour was just superb. In any case, as we had desks which could open, just as Mother Lucy flung the chalk, face red with anger, we all in unison opened the desks which meant the chalk broke and bounced off in a hundred directions, annoying her all the more. We all revelled in this. It seemed so hysterically funny and it took a long time for the laughter to subside. In retrospect I think we were total pains in the neck, and French was not Mother Lucy's subject, but she tried valiantly to get the fundamental pronunciation right and I will take the correct pronunciation of acute é to my deathbed. I was able to use French in my future travels to Laos and Vietnam where I visited and lived for some years and was complimented on my pronunciation – all thanks to the wonderful, heroic, long suffering dedication of Mother Lucy.

In higher years the school employed a lay French teacher, Madame Meyer Gleaves, to take our French classes even further. Madame was a sensation, an elegant lady, who being from Belgium, insisted that she come into each class speaking French. She brought with her the mystery and aplomb of Hercule Poirot, the Belgian detective from the Agatha Christie novels. She just appeared one day and from the first moment spoke to us in French. Our classes started with 'Bonjour mademoiselles' and we learned that French was still the most important language of the world even if it was being spoken less and less. But, deep down, if you really wanted to be civilised, you would speak French. I particularly liked the idea that French children, apparently, were given some chocolate every afternoon and thought this to be highly civilised behaviour.

We once drove Madame Meyer Gleaves to the heights of patriotic pride in a rousing rendition of the *Marseillaise* one Bastille Day. She asked if anyone would play it and by a process of elimination, the task fell to me. I ended up playing the melody on the piano with a few chords as everyone sang the *Marseillaise* at a special French 'event' at school. I performed drum rolls, just out of a whim, on the bottom notes of the piano, and entered into its spirit, with drum rolls that seemed to drive Madame to cry with sheer ecstasy – or was it pain? Strange to say, we never knew the true events surrounding July 14 in France, for it was a horrendous bloodbath for Christians and rather a black hole in world history. We merely heard that some prisoners were set free. I do not recall being told that thousands of priests and nuns were murdered and that it was a dark day for religious freedom. Perhaps it was mentioned but I do not recall it.

If not, I do not think there was any ideological intent there, simply a desire to avoid the unpleasant.

In other French classes, we all laughed as Madame read out excerpts of Molière's plays, especially *Le Bourgeois Gentilhomme*, as Madame kept bursting out into laughter herself as she read the passages. Her laughter was so infectious that we laughed because she laughed and she laughed because we laughed, not caring too much about the meaning of the French words.

But in counterpoint to the laughter of Molière, we also read Camus' *L'Etranger* which is a heavy work for 16-year-olds to grapple with, in terms of its ideas. We had to consider contemporary philosophical stances, and in this novel the main character is one for whom life is meaningless, for whom life was just like rolling a stone up a hill, watching it roll down, and then doing it again. We were stunned at being presented with such an empty world, bereft of metaphysical verities, so different from the one we knew. But we did not take it to heart, or at least I never did. We simply thought the main character pondered the meaning of existence.

We learned that Jean-Paul Sartre existed, that Albert Camus was influenced by him, and that Camus thought life was absurd, and tried to find his own unique meaning within these boundaries of absurdity. We learned about 'existentialist philosophy' and how some people seriously believed in it, though I truly could not fathom why. It did not strike me that such a view of the meaninglessness of existence could be true, as the weight of the meaningful Catholic legacy was so deeply imprinted, as was the struggle for survival and the ever present danger in Poland, the Baltic states and China which I was constantly hearing about. Feeling life was absurd was not an option when survival itself was at stake.

Nor did life seem absurd in the West at Brigidine, despite the culturally destabilising rise of the pop culture, the music of the

Beatles and the Rolling Stones, increasingly and pervasively played on every media outlet and the levity in *Jesus Christ Superstar* which took deliberate aim, it seemed to me, at the sacred. Things still rolled along at Brigidine despite the noise of the 'world' and the existentialists. So I merely felt sorry for Camus as I pondered his confrontation with death and the meaninglessness of life in *L'Etranger* and *La Peste* and grasped the issues, though I did not agree with the 'solution' of creating one's own moral universe.

When I came to study French at university, in the first term of the first year, we were presented with that very same existentialist philosophy, the works of Jean-Paul Sartre, Simone de Beauvoir and Camus, in retrospect, a sign of the atheist infiltration of much of the humanities that was gathering momentum in the 1970s. One of my first essays was on Jean-Paul Sartre, so as a gawky teenager just out of a Catholic school I sat down and wrote it.

As yet I had no idea how much a Communist supporter Sartre was, how much he supported the deconstruction of Western civilisation, seemed to pardon Soviet atrocities, or was an ardent atheist. Nor how much he inspired the *soixante-huitards*, those revolutionaries at the French barricades, how much he was behind the momentous cultural shift pervading the air around us as, for example, as outlined in Roger Scruton's *Fools, Frauds and Firebrands* (2017).

In my youthful naiveté, as a reffo kid, I just thought Sartre was an unhappy, miserable sort of person, who felt nauseous about a lot of things and mistreated Simone de Beauvoir. I read his work, read some critics, repeated some of the phrases I heard about him, and pleased the lecturer no end, but did not really understand the depth of the deconstruction he advocated until many years later.

The unforgettable, renowned music teacher, Mrs Mollie Watts, who taught at Brigidine in Randwick for several years. She studied with Sister Cecilia who studied with the Russian pianist Alexander Sverjensky.

17

MUSIC, TERROR AND RUSSIAN INFLUENCES

While I was never in that group of students who were proficient at Maths, as previously mentioned, there were many students who excelled at it. While they did their algebra and equations, I plodded along but, at the same time, was totally swept up into Brigidine's musical atmosphere, the wings of poesy and languages. In particular, I was inducted day by day into the music of the spheres as music seemed to envelop the school. Apart from general lessons in music, many had personal lessons and I became one of them. One enduring memory is that of students walking in a never-ending criss-crossing pattern across the school courtyards to go to their appointed teacher. There was a music section of the school, with about 10 separate small music rooms, all with musty airs and a piano in each. I recall that Mother Eymard, a renowned music teacher there, only ever considered a music student truly committed if she would give up her lunchtime and come in and practise with her left hand, while eating a sandwich with her right, and then changing hands. Music was a serious business.

I was encouraged to learn the piano, as were many girls in that era, and was assigned to one of the rare lay teachers at the school, Mrs Mollie Watts, as I was starting late. Here was another very interesting character at the school, a veritable tour de force, for Mollie Watts was a tall, vibrant Irish Catholic musician who could play four instruments and, as she related to us, 'topped the state in singing' in her A.Mus.A. She also played cello, violin and piano. She was a dynamo so, with this illustrious past, she taught part-time at Brigidine in an allocated room with a grand piano.

To enter this room with a grand piano, you crossed over into an enchanting world of music. It was a marvellously instructive and entertaining experience. Mrs Watts had lived in country towns in her youth and played piano, violin, cello and sang at various times in Condoblin, Forbes Leeton and other places, in which Celtic Australians all seemed to know each other. She said it was such 'fun' playing with her sisters in a lively but genteel band and would remark in her very dynamic way, 'It was the best time of my life'. She exuded an Irish breeziness and confidence about the world, and in this way, told me of Australian country life in a way I would otherwise not have heard about. She was the fiery essence of Irish Australia and of Ireland itself.

I was still introspective and rather shy at the beginning of my lessons, being more the nordic melancholic, dreamy, incommunicative type of person. The ebullient Mrs Watts could not understand this and would explode in frustration, threatening to throw me out of the room if I did not speak and overcome my shyness. Alas I was a useless article again, in terms of Irish sociability. This is no text-book way to treat shyness but Mrs Watts, whatever one's views of her methods, did eventually shock me into becoming more talkative through the sheer power of her incurably Irish optimistic personality. She continued to regale me with stories of the heroic Irish and country life in Australia in between my scales practice, Bach minuets and Beethoven pieces.

In this way I was inducted into Celtic thought as well as the world of music. She would say, 'That's a major fifth, as it starts just like the song, 'The Harp that once through Tara's Halls', as she sang some Irish song I had never heard of. She would say these things as if Moses were referring to the Commandments. Her students could not forget this lively certainty even if they tried, hence they always knew their intervals in their aural music exams, as they had the voice of Mollie Watts ringing in their ears, counting like a metronome and singing Irish songs to explain much besides. In later years I had occasion to visit Ireland and breathe in the atmosphere all the while recalling Mrs Mollie Watts and the wonderful nuns whose long story originated there.

Mrs Watts always said a prayer before each lesson at the piano and invoked the help of Saint Cecilia and other saints for all her students. This was normal for students of music in Catholic schools. As previously noted, there were saints for all situations, not only Saint Anthony for lost articles, Saint Catherine for headaches, St Thomas More for moral courage and so on. So it was as natural as breathing to invoke Saint Cecilia to help one play scales, arpeggios and do the 'lists' for the music exams, which were run by the Australian Music Examination Board (AMEB) at the school. Saint Cecilia was a highly placed ally.

The effervescent, highly talented Mrs Watts herself had studied under a nun whose name was Mother Cecilia, who was also very talented, and who had studied under one of the two famed Russian pianists in Sydney in her era, Alexander Sverjensky (1901-1971), who also taught the renowned Roger Woodward. This was of great significance, as Mother Cecilia passed on Sverjensky's 'technique' to Mrs Watts, who then taught her students a particular method of playing and made little musicians out of ungainly dolts like me. Thus, during the lesson, I would hear that the particular method of relaxing all the muscles and joints in the body came from this great man, Sverjensky, and much time would be spent attaining the physical and mental state required to play.

This was not yoga or Thi Chi, but a very effective way of attaining a kind of 'mindfulness' in order to focus on what one was doing. I had no idea at the time, but found out later that Sverjensky was born in Riga, Latvia, then under occupation, and part of the *Russian* Empire. So Mrs Watts had studied under someone whose roots went back to where my mother came from! The other pianist of great renown in Sydney at the time was Alexander Hmelnitsky (1891-1965) who was born in Kiev, then also part of the Russian Empire. Interestingly they both fled Communism, ended up in Australia and taught the lucky students who came their way, some of them Irish nuns. In the piano world, people belonged to one camp or another, and each regarded the other as heretical. I was irrevocably in the Sverjensky camp. Perish the thought that I would ever even dream of doing it Hmelnitsky's way!

Mrs Watts not only induced me to speak conversationally through sheer terror, but also shouted loudly that I should 'relax!' in no less terrorising a voice. She warned me that if I did not relax according to the methods of Mother Cecilia and the famed Sverjensky, I would be kicked out of the room forthwith and not ever be permitted to play a note. This was all part of her 'method'. With all this drama it took weeks of this concentration on 'relaxation' before I could put one finger on the keyboard. But this approach worked, and worked very well, as I think it focused the mind so much on the task of the moment. Many of her students, including myself, made rapid progress in the fundamentals of piano playing, which was the aim of the method. The little reffo kid was coming a long way playing Bach minuets and sonatas.

Perpetual music classes

Brigidine was feted for its music, from assemblies, choir and practice. I learned early on in high school that a former student, Helen Quach, had become a famous orchestral conductor, in fact, so we were told, the first of Chinese background (she was born in Vietnam of Chinese background) and had come to Brigidine before going to the Sydney conservatorium to study piano and violin. One of the most typical memories I have is of groups of students singing, practising and repeating musical phrases. I especially remember in third year, in a general music class, we had the task of analysing our

The music room at Brigidine where Mrs Mollie Watts, inheritor of the Sverjensky piano method, taught many students, where she shouted at me to 'relax', where endless scales and arpeggios were played up and down the pianos and where A.M.E.B. (Australian Music Examinations Board) exams were held. Here are the 8th Grade students in 1969: (left to right) Catherine Summerhayes, Diane Ray, yours truly, Carmel Pendergast and another schoolmate. While I did not become a composer, much to the surprise of Mrs Watts, many Brigidine students went on to distinguished music careers.

Music loomed large at Brigidine, with choirs, an orchestra and continual performances at concerts and assemblies. Here is a Brigidine Wind ensemble, circa 1965.

A more recent photo from the school showing the continuation of music making at Brigidine.

From my old song book from 1964-5. Whether of Australian, Chinese, Hungarian or Polish background, we sang of river banks, dales, braes and ash groves with refrains like 'Ri fol ri fol tole de ri riddle i do' and so on.

first concerto. Haydn's Trumpet Concerto was the chosen piece and we were told to learn the 'theme', a very memorable tune, so a few of us went around singing it 'pum, papum pa pumpa pumpa pum', along the corridors. The analysis was not too deep but it filled my consciousness for a while.

The school was filled with music practices for school assemblies and the orchestra practised each Friday afternoon. Articles were written about it and photos placed in the School Annuals.[32] I remember a talented girl Denise Grannall playing the flute with great skill and another, Jenny Ricketts, whose trombone was almost taller than she was. A multi-talented girl in our class, lovely Guilia Giuffré, seemed to be able to do everything, including playing the violin with great aplomb in the school orchestra. There were students often carrying cello, trumpet, violin and clarinet cases to and from lessons and performances. In fact the constancy of music practice, whether in groups or done singly, protected many children from the prevailing perils of adolescence as there was always something on the horizon to prepare for, practices, concerts, trials for exams – exams. We were always worried about the next music exam.

Music gives life perpetual purpose and is the cure for many ailments of adolescence, if not most of life in general, and every child should be given a chance to play a musical instrument of some kind, particularly in a brass band. It is a powerful psychological tool for engendering concentration and inner strength. In some it engendered great physical strength. I remember a fellow student, Phillipa Conway, one of the larger Conway family, could play the tuba so well at a young age that she had quite powerful lungs, as any tuba player would have. She played at school and told us about her scintillating experiences playing in various locales on the weekend in a brass band. She had sisters who played other musical instruments very well and told me there was a timetable in her house indicating who could practise at what time. Being an only child, I was truly impressed by the routines of a large family and admired the skills of the Conway girls. Phillipa once showed her physical prowess in a science class around 1967. Our science teacher told us one day how heavy mercury was and how, for example, no one would ever be able to blow it up this particular glass pipe. A few girls tried and proved the teacher's prediction correct as the mercury did not move. Then Phillipa was invited, too, and went up to the front of the class with a twinkle in her eye. She was able to demonstrate her formidable pulmonary strength and blow the mercury way up the pipe to the amazement of all. That's what playing the tuba could do. It could defy the laws of science! Or almost – much to our amazement. Phillipa was a mainstay of the school orchestra and once, unless my memory fails me, later played with the Elizabethan Orchestra and either she or someone she knew learnt to play 'The Flight of the Bumble Bee' on the tuba.

If you ask me about nostalgic memories of sport, I do not have any as I quickly lost interest in team sports, athletics and so on. But Brigidine had great tennis, basketball and softball teams. They had marching teams which were judged on their marching prowess. One of my friends, Robyn O'Hearn-Maciejewski, whom I met in later years and attended Santa Sabina in Strathfield, had talent in this area and showed me her 'sports' photographs. Sport was a world on its own in most schools, just as the other subjects were. Robyn, however, was good at everything, maths, music and sport – you name it. She ended up being the musical director at Marian Valley in Queensland, a Catholic pilgrimage site, a position she still holds to this day. She has theatrical and musical ability, of great value at a place visited by thousands of pilgrims. But no matter which sport she tried, she took to it like a duck to water. Now, whenever we meet we discuss our past Catholic educations which were so similar though in different schools.

For me, as I said, sport is like a black hole, especially the world of tennis. I recall Mrs Mollie Watts forbidding any of her students from learning tennis as this would interfere with piano students developing equally balanced strength in each hand. In fact if you were in her music world, you had to forsake many other activities as she not only taught music, but induced her students to live and breathe it. Mrs Watts was nearly on a par with Moses and Ezechiel being a 'she who must be obeyed'.

I also remember that there were students very gifted in maths and science who were deeply engrossed in formulae and had ambitions to study medicine, become scientists and so on. One talented student, Susan Delfandahl, was quick at solving problems we could not, and she went on, unless I am mistaken, to become a medical doctor. Paula Quirk went on to do science, as did several other students. I, on the other hand, had no such ambitions, could not stand the sight of blood and was squeamish, so remained with my music and poetry.

I remember clearly a girl from my year, Carmel Pendergast, playing the violin so exquisitely that it drew tears from my eyes, especially her playing of the second movement of Mendelssohn's Violin Concerto which I had ringing in my ears for a long time. Another girl, Mary Mackel, played the viola in a beguiling, mellow way and was determined to get into an orchestra – which she did. She also joined the Elizabethan Orchestra at some point after leaving school. It was with Mary Mackel that occurred one of the strangest incidents of my school life. Many music students were encouraged to dabble in composing pieces of music at Brigidine. For me composing was as easy as solving equations was for maths students, so I got the bright idea that Mary might agree to play some of my highly angst-filled, teenage melodies, which I wrote for viola, while I played rippling arpeggio accompaniment up and down the piano – 'molto leggerio et doloroso'. Mary was gracious enough to play them too and we had great fun.

Somehow, from hearing these pieces, my music teacher became convinced I might become a musical composer though this was the last thing on my mind. I was induced to write a composition for the Composition Contest in our final year of school which of course I did as it was easy for me. I wrote this viola piece which Mary played with great panache. It was very gloomy and full of such dramatic, rippling arpeggios that to my amazement, this piece led to my winning the contest. There was a large assembly for general prize giving looming. My parents came but were rather puzzled as my being a musical composer had never been among their plans for their daughter, and neither had it ever crossed my mind. But there you go; the nuns, Mrs Watts and some classmates were all convinced I would be one. My parents, though puzzled, were nonetheless pleased as the famed Australian composer Werner Baer gave me the prize.

This prize fuelled my music teacher's inordinate desire that I *would* become a composer and she went to the lengths of arranging an interview with Werner Baer himself, after the concert, thinking we could engage in esoteric 'composer talk' which would launch me on my way to stardom. I remember travelling to the city with a leaden heart not knowing exactly why I was going. Then I found myself sitting in Werner Baer's room at the Conservatorium, frozen and incommunicative. I did not know really what to say, though he was gracious enough with the teenager before him, and perhaps thought my quietness a sign of artistic depth, though it was not, it was just embarrassment. I walked out of the interview with such relief. But try as I might, I could not dissuade Mrs Watts from her vision of my future as a composer until I was older.

In the end I did not become a composer, rather I studied education, psychology, languages and literature at university. Despite all this, I am eternally grateful to Mrs Watts for her irrepressible confidence in her students, her unforgettable personality, and her unique and dynamic approach as a gifted music teacher. As a music teacher, she was one in a million.

Singing about ash groves, Erin's isle and prison chains

As I said previously, singing songs with an Anglo-Celtic provenance had been a big part of primary school and now we continued with such songs in high school. I recall clearly singing about English ash trees without ever having seen such a tree:

> The ash grove how graceful, how plainly 'tis speaking
> The wind through it playing has language for me.
> When over its branches the sunlight is breaking,
> A host of kind faces is gazing at me.
> The friends from my childhood again are before me
> Each step brings a memory as freely I roam.
> With soft whispers laden the leaves rustle o'er me
> The ash grove, the ash grove alone is my home.

Not only did we sing about ash trees, we also sang about Afton water among the 'green braes', about Richmond Hill, Strawberry Fair and 'Hark hark the lark', ringing out choruses with 'fah, lah lah lah lah' and 'tir-a-lee tir-a-loo' And so on. While few of us had seen the ash, chestnut or maple trees so highly feted in these songs, in this way we continued to acquire our Anglo-Celtic inheritance and now, many years later, as a tribute to the success of this transmission, I can still sing some of the above songs under my breath and still possess the old songbook. Of course, we also sang the school song to St Brigid all throughout my schooldays and I know it from memory, imagining 'Erin's isle' as a shining green jewel in the sea somewhere:

> Far above enthroned in glory
> Sweetest Saint of Erin's Isle

See thy children kneel before thee
Turn on us a Mother's smile.

Sancta Mater, hear our pleading
Faith and hope and holy love
Sweet St Brigid, spouse of Jesus,
Sent to us from Heaven above.

Sweet St Brigid, Erin's children,
Far and near o'er land and sea
In the world and in the cloister
Fondly turn with love to thee.

Sancta Mater, sooth the mourner
Shield the weary tempted soul
Sweet St Brigid, guide thy children
To thy bright and happy home.[33]

It turns out that the words of this song were composed by a Sister Cecilia in 1911, although I don't know whether it is the same nun who taught Mollie Watts, as many nuns were named after this great musical saint. We also sang to 'Hail glorious St Patrick, dear saint of our isle' and asked him to bestow on us, his poor children, a sweet smile. We sang as if we would know the words forever, believing these songs had existed for all eternity and that everyone else knew them. Years later I taught in a state school as I was appointed there to 'pay off' my Teachers' College Scholarship and was amazed that they sang a Latin refrain to their school song 'Ad astra'. Mother Conleth our Latin teacher was right, Latin could be found everywhere, and was not dead yet.

All throughout school, I recall regular visits to the local church, Our Lady of the Sacred Heart in Randwick, to sing hymns at Mass. At this time we were still part of the era of feast day marches at the school, with banners everywhere, the Children of Mary and those aspiring to be one ('Aspirants'), the Sodalities and St Vincent de Paul. We had the 'Living Parish' hymn book, in which were 'Soul of My Saviour', 'Hail Queen of Heaven', 'To Jesus Heart all Burning' and of course, the often sung 'Pange Lingua' in Latin. I came to learn them from memory, such was the effect of regular singing. We sang the song which would make feminists blanche, 'Faith of Our Fathers Living Still', with great gusto:

> Our fathers chained in prisons dark,
> Were still in heart and conscience free.
> How sweet would be their children's fate,
> If they like them could die for Thee

For a child of refugees who had family in the gulags, while it was nice to sing of 'ash trees', this was a finer and more fitting song to defeat the forces arraigned against Catholicism in the twentieth century and beyond. This was no mere triumphalism, no 'old style Catholicism' to be superseded, to be scorned as quaint, but described a real and present battle between the destructive forces of Communism and our Catholic heritage, of which I had become ever more aware, especially as regards those imprisoned around the world because of it. Then we sang in martial rhythm 'We Stand for God and for His Glory, the Lord Supreme and God Most High'. These hymns depicted a world of meaning with which I easily identified, because of my personal family history, It seemed a perfectly reasonable and necessary part of Catholic life to sing them, not seeming part of a musty past at all. How little I understood that within a decade many of these hymns would have disappeared from some local churches forever and my sense of ever present danger, in terms of a cultural war, was on the right track.

The school orchestra played on many occasions and there were even ex-students who came to join in sometimes. I remember a girl holding up a trombone which was taller than she was when it was fully pulled out!

Helen Quach (1940-2013), born in Vietnam, attended Brigidine College, Randwick, and went on to become a renowned orchestral conductor studying under Sir John Barbirolli in Italy and becoming assistant to Leonard Bernstein in New York. She conducted many orchestras and founded the Kuringai Symphony Orchestra in Sydney

18

ORDER AND DISORDER IN THE COSMOS

For most of its students, despite the anti-authoritarian protests and political unrest of the 1960s in America and France, Brigidine Convent school reflected some kind of prevailing order of the universe. It threaded the days of lessons, music exams, sport and assemblies. No doubt this is true of many people's memories of their schooldays but it seemed even more so for me in retrospect, even if there were challenging voices and people leaving religious orders. Events might come and go, revolutions, conflicts and disarray, things might look disoriented but all would settle back into the ordered cosmos that had been ordained for all time in the Catholic world, in Benedictine, Franciscan and Trappist monasteries and in that outpost called Brigidine Convent. As we walked up stairs, we were obliged to offer to carry books or bags for nuns if we encountered them, we were to help them clean up at ends of terms, stand up for older passengers on buses and wear hats and gloves on the streets. It was forbidden to eat on the streets in uniform and, as the Eastern suburbs were then still very Irish Catholic, students might be 'reported' for misdemeanours by onlookers and residents.

So strong was this sense of order and propriety that one day the girls in my fifth form (now called Year 11) had to deal with a dramatic event. A nun solemnly announced the bad news that, 'a Brigidine girl was seen eating grapes at Coogee beach in school uniform yesterday'. We were horrified. It was such a loathsome act, clearly compromising the reputation of the school. This led to a declaration that the entire class would be kept in after school until the girl owned up. And so it transpired – we were kept in, for these sorts of things happened in those days. We sat at our desks quietly staring ahead of us in solemn reflection on this dastardly act, in this war of nerves. We stared at the displeased nun, and she stared at us. Time passed slowly, tensions rose ever higher. Then the guilty girl broke down, revealed herself and confessed her crime. She was led out of class sobbing to the senior nun who was going to 'deal with her'. But punishments were largely innocuous, though annoying to us, mainly detentions and confessions of one's crime and getting notes sent home.

For a while we had a system of receiving good and bad marks for our deeds in order to encourage us to do good and avoid the bad. We had to tally them at the end of the week and the house group with the most marks got approbation and applause. This worked well until one of the retired nuns with dementia, Mother Gertrude, a very sweet person who walked around the playground at times, gave out thousands and even millions of good marks to anyone she encountered. We loved Mother Gertrude and went out of our way to meet her and acquire millions of moral riches this quick, easy way showing a certain opportunism or turpitude on our parts! The system obviously could not withstand the generosity of this kind nun. So it did not last long and good and bad marks were abandoned.

While I spoke little at school of the post-war shadows that lay over my life, there was a sense in the school nonetheless that both Communism and Nazism were evil, that one was lucky to have survived, that is, if one's parents had survived these things, and that 'the West was best'. This was part of the vision of 'order' in the Brigidine cosmos, at least that is how I perceived it, so we felt part of the civilised West, on the right side of things in the Cold War. The fellow East Europeans my parents met knew only too well the threat Communism posed once its roots were planted in a country.

Mother Mark, who was a principal at Brigidine for a number of years.

The final year class at Brigidine in 1969, with Mother Justin, standing with us all. She was, like the other nuns, greatly admired and loved, hard-working and encouraged us in what we did.

In whimsical mood, a cheerful group of school leavers on their last day at school in 1969.

An excursion I cannot remember towards the end of our school days, clearly a happy, summery, breezy occasion. Left to right: Myself, Julianne Golby, Maureen Power, Guilia Giuffré, Philippa Conway (the latter of extraordinary tuba playing fame).

They were not involved in politics, although they liked the sound of the Liberal Party and the DLP, but had suspicions about the Labor Party. One Polish immigrant working at the Ford Factory in Sydney had to endure his union boss being a declared Communist which he had come to via the Labor Party. My parents did not know of the earlier anti-Communist efforts of Father Paddy Ryan to counteract Communist propaganda, by means of public talks in many places in Australia, but they would have loved him if they had done so. James Franklin describes Father Ryan's activities well in his superb account entitled *Catholic Values and Australian Realities* (2006).[34] For example in 1948, Fr Ryan debated 'That Communism is in the best interests of the Australian people' with Edgar Ross, a member of the central committee of the Communist Party of Australia. As Franklin says, despite the rain, 30,000 turned up. The audience, including nuns, laughed derisively at Ross, accusing him of pulling the wool over their eyes with his Communist claims of offering 'human rights', and being 'strong, secure stable and prosperous'. Fr Paddy Ryan was able to give ample evidence of the opposite and of the abuse of human rights in the Soviet Union on a scale unimaginable in the West. Fr Paddy Ryan won the day, and had my parents been there (they were at the time too busy escaping Communism), they would have cheered him on too.

There were hints of Christian martyrdom beyond the Brigidine world, especially in eastern Europe and China. But as yet I knew nothing then of the betrayals of the West perpetrated by those who had benefited from it. One of the most salient examples of such betrayal, by those who attended 'good schools', were no doubt Philby, Burgess and Maclean, Blunt and Cairncross, the Cambridge Five. They, and many others swept along with utopianism, became Soviet agents in the 1930s in the West, betraying many agents and causing their deaths. Much has been written of them. One of the Cambridge Group, Anthony Blunt, became a British knight, art historian and Surveyor of the King's Pictures, and later the Queen's Pictures before confessing his treason – in 1964 – and was later stripped of his honours. I mention this to say that while I lived in that wonderful, ordered Brigidine universe, the 'Western world' as many perceived it, was being undermined and attacked in many ways, often by those who had profited from its educational, social and political benefits. At that tender age in Brigidine, I did not grasp the nature of this anti-Western, anti-colonialist and anti-Christian sentiment and the looming waves of moral relativism, post-modernism or secular humanism that were on the horizon. But they were beginning to sweep through the institutions of the Western world. Recognising cultural Marxism was a long way off. Here in Randwick, it seemed all made sense, and would do so forever.

In senior high school we were warned, however, against studying philosophy at university in the future as we would 'lose the faith', though this seemed inconceivable to us. But evidently the nuns were on to something. There were dangers 'out there'. We had no idea of the philosophical assaults on the Christian worldview which had grown since the time of the Enlightenment, the deconstruction of Christian belief already proceeding apace in the secular universities, described so well, again by James Franklin in *Corrupting the Youth: A History of Philosophy in Australia* (2003).[35] We simply knew we lived in the 1960s, full of promise for a future which could only get better. Surely people had learned the lessons of war? My family had come from Eastern Europe, kept hearing of the horrors 'over there' which affected them personally but strove to make a better life. They had worked hard and done well, my father who had risen in rank at the Water Board where he worked, made friends, had wisdom, had a unique incisive humour and was an avid reader. My mother, despite illness, kept helping people when she could and humbly walked her 'via Crucis' in this life. Both parents had rich gifts of the mind and heart and came to have friends of all nationalities. Babcia remained an example of endurance and warmth in the lives of all she met. One of her menial jobs was to iron clothes for a Jewish lady with whom she became such friends that the 'work' part was dropped and they just met to talk. They had survived the Holocaust and had much to share. They both thought it was good to be in Australia, and surely, they thought, surely, people could see through socialist and other grand utopias and never bring them here.

More revelry on the last day at Brigidine with Christine McNab (below, centre) in playful mood.

19

Rumours of Revolution,
The End of an Era

It did transpire in my senior years, 1968-9, that, along with the sense of an ordered cosmos, a strange new atmosphere began wafting through the school corridors. I recall the day we all sat in a science laboratory and watched the first man walk on the moon and that there was a sense of 'anything is possible now'. But it was more than that. There was an indefinable hint of limitless progress mixed with hope, an intangible sense of 'something from somewhere' which we could not understand and hence had no way of recognising for what it was. And so many of my thoughts expressed here are with some reflections and conclusions drawn in hindsight.

Suddenly new religious and political 'issues' of the day crept into discussion in Religion classes. We were living in the era of 1968, that watershed year of the twentieth century, the year of the promulgation of the encyclical *Humanae Vitae* (1968), the year often taken as the beginning of the cultural revolution in the West. Students asked questions about what contraception and abortion were and we were told by the nuns they were unambiguous evils, even though, as I now understand, there was widespread dissent on these subjects in other parts of the world. Fr Paddy Ryan, of anti-Communist debating fame, said in 1968, however, that there was no possibility of a Catholic disagreeing in conscience with this encyclical – a year before he died in 1969.[36] At Brigidine, one nun told us confidently that 'abortion will never come to Australia' and that euthanasia was a strange thing, confined to science fiction novels, so we need not worry on that score. As for gay marriage, many of us did not even know what a homosexual was. But in a vague way, something was looming, hints of some cultural cracks we could not clearly see; the silver clouds seemed to have dark linings.

At the same time we had a visiting teacher from what was known then as the Aquinas Academy who gave a series of talks on Thomistic philosophy – a short series – presumably to protect us from strong currents of anti-religious philosophies prevailing at secular universities. Alice Nelson, a young philosophy lecturer from that institute was invited by the nuns to introduce us to some traditional philosophical ideas. Interestingly, many years later I went back to this institute, later named the Centre for Thomistic Studies, which held classes in the city and enjoyed the other courses they offered. But at school we were just fledgling philosophers, whose ponderings were mixed with the infallibilities of youth. But we learned to separate 'substance' from 'accident' and pondered the 'essence' of things. This was part of the preparation for going 'out there ... into the world' which would be fraught with unexpected dangers.

Little did we know that post-modernist thought, successor to the Enlightenment, waged war on the legacy of Western philosophy and theology and rejected its truths. We had knowledgeable and kind teachers like Mother Justin in our final year, giving her own example of being intelligent, reasonable and loyal to our Catholic faith, giving an example of the enduring sanity of the Christian worldview. We had Mother Conleth bequeathing us a kind of scepticism about all things worldly, and Mother Loyola reminding us always of the eternal present. We had been 'formed' to challenge and question the post-modernists. It seemed that the nuns still had a strong sense of the Catholic universe even if it was under assault. Yes, things were changing.

Little could I, or anyone at Brigidine, imagine in the slightest the coming persecution of Christians in the West within a few decades, initially by insidious infiltration, and later by the increasing coercion of political correctness where one could be vilified simply for saying things like 'marriage is between a man and a woman' and for whom the touchstone of progressive correctness would be support for abortion. This was a far cry from the worldview of Mother Pascal. It awaited us like a sword of Damocles over our heads.

Jolly songs appear at Mass

In 1969, my final year, we would still walk to Mass through the streets of Randwick to the church of Our Lady of the Sacred Heart – now a basilica, filled with beautiful altars and statues. I recall the day we students, seated before Mass, were asked to sing what seemed a strange song – *Spirit of God in the Clear Running Water* – for, as one nun put it, this is 'what the Bishops want now'; and as most Catholics had a trust in authority and the hierarchy of the Church, we sang it. Mother Conleth, however, seemed to suspect such changes and she showed it in her 'non verbals'. She had taught us about Caesar's wars but here were the suspicious signs of a differing kind of war – perhaps she saw the attempt to 'modernise' as a guerrilla attack on Western culture, in particular our Catholic inheritance. Perhaps others had differing attitudes at the time, but I was aware of some subterranean disquiet.

I remember there was a half-heartedness with which the new songs were announced at Mass. But despite this uneasy tone, we were encouraged to sing jolly songs about Holy Communion and sacred things. We did sound jolly, but in a lacklustre way.

For me, it seemed as if we were all caught in some kind of strange web. This is not to point any finger at anyone but to observe that some certainly saw the jolly songs as a new opening and new style but some did not.

This lacklustre mood certainly washed over me, creating some cognitive dissonance, for the jolliness somehow conflicted with the sense of the sacred we had been bequeathed thus far. But we did it all in obedience, in the way theologian Tracey Rowland spoke of many Catholics at the time having an 'undue deference' to authority, that is to those way beyond the parish school boundaries.[37] Her view was that the authoritative tone seemed to shift from a tradition-conserving one to a change-focused one. Rowland adds that in the decades to come, it had an 'infantilising' effect on some congregations. One particular song which conveyed to me a conflict between jolliness and the sacred, stays in memory and I wince when I recall it sung in a quick four-step dance-like rhythm:

> Sons of God, hear his holy word,
> Gather round the table of the Lord,
> Eat his Body, Drink his Blood,
> And we'll sing a song of love,
> Allelu, Allelu, Allelu, Alleluuu -uuu aa -

I recall feeling somewhat dispirited but there was nowhere for the dispirited feelings to go, no template that would make sense of them. Along with the sense of cracks in the edifice of all I had known in terms of church music, there was nevertheless a heady sense of progress which no-one could deny, and much of it good. For these were the dramatic years, especially of medical discoveries and means of mass help for refugees, which opened doors of boundless confidence in social progress. If we could walk on the moon, surely we could progress in every way, even in church songs. Of course progress is good if it helps people, but change for change's sake has always been a debatable proposition. Progress can be genuine reform or can mask deeper changes which can have the destabilisin effects on a society.

For a while our religious classes were put into the hands of a priest who rode up to school on a motor bike in 1968 to speak to us about 'issues'. This struck many as very 'modern', cool and perhaps a sign of things to come. We now knew there was an event called 'Vatican II' and saw glimpses of the opening procession with its 2,800 bishops (making it the largest and most international gathering in the history of the Church) with its 400 *periti*, experts assisting the bishops, with almost as many journalists as bishops. We did not know that the more extroverted *periti* had created a virtual conference by engaging the media and that, as Woodward puts it, 'were mostly reclusive scholars, more at home in small seminars than at press conferences', so extroverted personalities and naive optimism won the day.[38] It was still clear to us that it had happened very far away. Still, in the late 1960s, we had no doubt the Pope was in charge of everything and momentary glitches would be ironed out. We knew that some kind of social force was gyrating and getting ever closer but had no idea what it meant. We could not understand then what Aidan Nichols called the over-optimistic cultural expectations of many Council attendees:

> ... a sense of optimism that world culture and the values cherished by the Church were on an increasingly convergent course.[39]

While Brigidine still constituted a secure and familiar world, it seems in retrospect – and I am talking of the wider society here – that the Church's values which it represented, and those of 'the world' were on a collision course, perhaps even more so than depicted in Augustine's *City of God*.

What was going on?

Some may disagree with me but it seemed as if the Western world was caught up in an overwhelming belief in *progress* at the expense of understanding of the human capacity for evil. In the past that heretical group called the Pelagians had sidelined the human capacity for evil. Of course, I did not know what Pelagian, semi-Pelagian or deconstruction meant at the time, but in later years, some used these words in describing the spirit of the times. During my university years I saw peers – not specifically Brigidine students, but University students in general – naively drawn into just such Pelagian, utopian movements of political salvation, spouting leftist/ Marxist views, seeing sin as 'social' not 'personal.' Often the lack of a spiritual formation easily led to political world building. My Brigidine education had given immunity to such utopianism. Marx and Carl Rogers were weaving their notions into Western institutions as American writer Paul Kengor explains well of this era.[40]

There were some Catholics who were drawn into the laudable aim of wanting to 'help the world' as social justice was an ideal for them. Many, however, had no way of critically assessing some of the good ideals against the quasi-Marxist political gospels floating around them. I stood on the sidelines watching peers, who had never experienced Communism close at hand, being swept away by Marxist style ideas of building a new society and excoriating the old. It certainly stunned me. My scepticism about this quasi-Marxist social justice hype was aroused and I 'sensed' what was happening, even if I could not put words to it.

How could it be otherwise? For this child, whose parents had lost their countries and families because of 'social justice' Communist utopias based on Marx and Lenin, this approaching post-Conciliar focus on earthly justice alone wore a suspicious mask. Were Marxist notions being disguised as evangelical zeal? Even if I did not know that this was indeed the case, and astutely manipulated by Soviet purse strings as we know now, I had some kind of 'instinct' about it.[41] The 'spirit' of Vatican II seemed a 'mantra', always seemed submerged beneath very earthly plans, very optimistic verbiage and the contemplative dimension of our earlier school years was giving way to increasingly confident political plans to help the world, even if the plans were dubious and did not help the world. I realise this is no doubt different from the way some others saw it but there were well-founded reasons for thinking this way.

Some characterised the assaults on the Western world's Christian heritage by the term 'cultural Marxism' which was aligned with social control beneath the social transformations disguised as 'progress'. While Communism had appeared for a long time to be 'over there', it would have been unheard of even to suggest it could infiltrate Western societies. But the increasing evidence of European Marxist intellectuals, like Marxists Antonio Gramsci, Herbert Marcuse and Georg Lukacs, and their influence at mainstream universities, certainly leads to unsettling questions in hindsight. In our Brigidine world, I would venture to say that few saw what was happening as cultural Marxism – certainly I did not. In hindsight, however, I can see there was an attack on what Marxists call the cultural 'superstructure', that is, society's religious base, whose effects are evident today, however one may account for the causes.[42] Brigidine was one of the last lines of defence of this cultural superstructure.

It was years later that I learned of Italian Communist Antonio Gramsci's envisioned attack on Western society, a long march through the society's institutions – including the judiciary, the military, the schools, the media – and Christianity. He concluded that so long as the workers had a Christian soul, they would not respond to revolutionary appeals hence the soul transmitted through a good Catholic education was to be a target, namely the kind transmitted at Brigidine would be the target of the post-modernist assault whose enemy was any past coherent view of the universe. As the song goes, we were on the 'eve of destruction'.

Awaiting us were waves of criticism, so-called Critical Theory which praised anything 'other' than the West and reinterpreted it in terms of class, race and gender. Beneath disguises of 'renewal' many did not understand that the strident atheist views could be transformed into more beguiling, spiritually toxic versions of 'values', leading to the stranglehold of politically correct virtues of 'marriage equality,' 'euthanasia', 'limitless freedom' and 'choice' as regards controlling life and death.[43]

Doubtless, because of my background, the Vietnam anti-war marches at the time also seemed puzzling to me, not that I was pro any war, but I had some inkling of the way that Soviet disinformation might work its deceptions in ways young Western protestors would not understand. To see people pro Ho Chi Minh was very puzzling. Time has proven this view correct as there was constant Soviet disinformation fed to the youth in the West in this era as several high ranking defectors from the Soviet Union explained.[44] I had grown up with parents who were the victims of Communism, of Yalta, and my instincts told me that continual calls for 'renewal' were suspicious – like the language of agitprop used in *Pravda*. Renewal, progress and change can be good. But one is permitted to question: Renewal to what end? Progress to where? Change for what reason? How could I think otherwise? We rejoiced in the 1960s when my great uncle Stanislaus was released from a gulag in the Soviet Union barely alive. We heard continually of those who did not survive. How could we champion cultural Marxism?

One who was there

I am aware that nothing is guaranteed to create a storm as much as if one tries to say something about the 1960s, as I have above, for memories, views and conclusions differ, and, in the end, there is much more that could be said. But I am not alone in thinking that despite our solid, wide-ranging education at Brigidine, the West was on the brink of being torn apart by destructive cultural attacks at the time I attended school. A person who went overboard with the 60s Marxist *Zeitgeist* in the West and then 'woke up' was German writer Peter Seewald. He was born a Catholic, was carried away by the anti-institutional ambience of the times and then decades later saw through his own and the era's delusions. He experienced it all in Germany much earlier than it hit the Antipodes where we were sailing through a largely calm Catholic education singing 'Faith of our Fathers' and 'We Stand for God and for His Glory'. Seewald was simply drawn into the 'power and madness' of the times, of the strong belief in a 'progressive society', namely a false notion of progress, as were so many of his Western peers. It derived more from centrifugal social forces, which affected Vatican II, rather than being 'caused' by Vatican II. But Seewald was honest enough to leave the illusions behind when he learned of the atrocities carried out in Soviet Eastern Europe (unlike many who clung to the illusions, like Sartre, even after confronted with Marxist/ Communist societies' brutal realities). Seewald was to become the famed author of several books which make for fascinating reading, notably those in which he conducted lengthy interviews with Pope Benedict XVI as Pope and Emeritus Pope. The latter trusted Seewald's understanding of what had transpired in the second half of the twentieth century well enough to feel he was conversing with a friend. Seewald stated:

> During the student rebellions of 1968 I began to engage with politics. Christianity seemed something of a relic from the past then. I felt that its mixture of power and madness had to be overcome in order finally to build a genuinely progressive society. So one day I withdrew myself from the Church. I felt liberated, and I fought for the ideas of Marx and Lenin. Now, with the passage of time, I've left Communism behind me. We did not know then what atrocities and millions of victims Maoism left behind in China (or rather, we did not want to know), but it was clear to me that these ideological systems cannot be reconciled with human dignity.[45]

Many saw Christianity as a 'relic from the past' and, like Seewald, 'fought for the ideas of Marx and Lenin'. Part of the era's sense of heady 'liberation' was also to come from humanist psychology, with its focus on self-actualisation, promulgated by Carl

Rogers, Abraham Maslow and their peers. The West was awash with therapeutic ideas and people sought themselves any way they could, as Joyce Milton writes perceptively in her book about the 1960s and 70s, *The Road to Malpsychia* (2002). There was in humanistic psychology the notion that psychological/religious change will arise, if one understands that institutions and religious beliefs are 'a shackle' and that one has to throw them off. I disagreed with these notions so much it drove me to write a doctorate on the subject. And I had the memory of nuns, priests and others who had bequeathed reason and memory, two precious gifts of the Western legacy, which helped us against the brewing cultural attacks on Christianity.

At the very same time that I was attending school in the 1960s, Rogers' colleague, William Coulson, was trying out Roger's theories in Catholic schools in the United States. Coulson, who later broke away from Rogers, was saying that he used his (Coulson's) Catholic connections to gain access to some Catholic schools. This was in order to try Rogers' humanistic, psychological self-focused methods as an experiment on those who did not require any psychological help. At the Californian Immaculate Heart of Mary convent, where the new psychologists spoke regularly to nuns of the new self-actualisation, Coulson says the end result of this psychological program, called the 'Education Innovation Program', was an amazing decimation of almost the entire order. The focus on self and spirit of rebellion against religious institutions was an intended consequence, for 'inner' development, though the near annihilation of the religious order was not. He says:

> When we started the project which was called one in educational innovation, there were 600 nuns and 59 schools: a college, eight high schools and fifty elementary schools. Now four years later as I write, a year following the formal completion of the project, there are two schools left and no nuns. We did some job.[46]

This type of psycho-social experiment in schools did not hit Australia at the time I was at Brigidine, or if it did, it went right over my head and I saw nothing. There were still nuns around who taught so marvellously well, prayers mattered, there was reverence, seriousness and a sense of the eternal. There were no shackles in my Catholic education that I felt I had to throw off. Looking back, my view is similar that of theologian David Schindler who wrote about the deeply spiritual *communio* within the Church being the agent of the culture's transmission and society's transformation. That *communio*, he said, arises from its understanding of the Trinity and the Incarnation – which we had in abundance. From this emanates the spiritual solidarity that informs all other types of relationships and union within the Church. It transformed Western society before, it can do so again.[47] We had that *communio* for most of the 1960s; it formed us and was taught to us from day one.

No-one at Brigidine, and few in Australia or the West, knew of even more remarkable events going on 'out there' pertaining to Fr Karol Wojtyła, that acute, visionary defender of Western values, lecturing in a Lublin University under Soviet Poland during the 1960s, exactly at the time when I attended school. Actually Lublin Catholic University (the Katolicki Uniwersytet Lubelski – known as KUL) was not far from where my father was born and where my Polish cousins lived. I was fortunate enough to be able to visit it and see the room where Father Wojtyła lectured, with its simple table, chairs and blackboard. In this Communist world were growing the seeds of a remarkable other revolution which would overthrow the Soviet empire. Such distance, such closeness, such parallel universes existed at the time: one with Wojtyła, soon to be pope, defending the Western legacy in Communist Poland; and the post-modern one about to deconstruct the Christian West.

In fact the extraordinary story of Fr Wojtyła's elevation to the papacy as Pope John Paul II had a profound effect on Eastern

Europeans who had fled Communism and had come to the West. I remember the day he was elected in 1978, just as I remembered the assassination of President Kennedy. My grandmother seemed to think the Vatican had come to its senses in electing a Polish Pope at last! Not to mention that this election seemed to have a profound effect on people of every nation in the world, for all sensed they were living through some great historical moment, that something grand was afoot, as did I. And so did the Communist leadership when they saw the millions gather for Pope John Paul II's return to Poland in 1979. Some feared the power of spiritual cohesion, and intuitively sensed the looming collapse of their political utopia.

Here was a spiritual realist challenging one of the world's most repressive regimes with a deeply spiritual 'communio'. Spiritual communio confronted Marxism and communio won! When I was in St Peter's Square years later at the canonisation of this Pope who had stood up to the Soviet empire, I wondered why he had touched people from all corners of the globe. As I was to write of the canonisation for the Catholic journal *Annals*, I spoke to various groups of people in that heady, spiritually charged atmosphere of those days. I asked a group of Ugandans why they liked the new saint. They responded simply, 'He understood us' and I pondered that for a long time, after hearing similar answers from others. It seems the Pope/saint was not only in tune with the Soviet world, but deeply and broadly sensed the sufferings of others in all kinds of political, social and personal strife. His very eyes communicated something of the 'suffering servant', of mercy itself, his heart spoke to hearts. He drew all into this spiritual unity that had sustained him, the one that had drawn me too at the schools run by nuns, the spiritual communio that was puncturing the post-modern agenda. Saint John Paul II had laid the foundations of a post-post-modern solidarity, a developing counter-revolution standing up to cultural Marxism. And he was doing it, while we Brigidine students were doing our exams and thinking of the future.

20

PARTING WITH AN ABIDING RICH HERITAGE ...

Back in 1969, after years of music, French, poetry and Caesar's wars, we students at Brigidine found ourselves almost grown up. The final year of school had arrived. I began to believe, finally, this child of refugees and 'useless article' might make good. I looked to doing the final exams and in this way giving pleasure to my refugee parents though my mother was very ill at the time and I was wracked with worry. Attending university still seemed a noble, exalted aim, despite the warnings about philosophy and the fact that I might *not* be a musical composer. I thought I might be able to do an Arts degree at Sydney University if I got a Commonwealth or Teachers' Scholarship (I did). Such were the dreams of many baby boomers like myself in that hopeful 60s era, despite the social and political disquiet around us. My mother did get better for a while and my exam results did give my parents joy, that I had 'made it' – as happened with many other parents.

There we stood with hair in long pony tails fluttering in the wind, as tall as the nuns walking in corridors, in school grounds and under gum, Moreton Bay and palm trees, saying 'serious' things about our futures and facing the final test of our minds. Karel, Esther, Francis and Mary and other classmates all had plans to do many interesting things. Somehow it all happened so quickly as we moved to the parting edges of youth and on to 'the rest of our lives'. We had had Year 10 and Year 12 balls, with bands like the Easybeats playing in person and the music of Billy Thorpe and the Aztecs not to mention

Angels, Incense and Revolution: Catholic Schooldays of the 1960s

Ray Brown and the Whispers playing in the background. But that was all past for now we journeyed with optimistic hearts across that strange horizon with its mix of anxieties and hopeful dreams, mystery and enigma. Here the line was especially poignant, as the cultural ground was giving way and we were virtually final witnesses to an era where the Judeo-Christian worldview, which had held some sway among Australians, was about to be attacked on all sides.

In the 1960s we were, perhaps, a bit behind the times at St Brigid's and Brigidine. Hence my memories in the preceding chapters are rather of the old world, the positive legacies of Western Christendom which the nuns so successfully passed on. During the coming decades, I never felt 'downtrodden' or 'oppressed' as some reformers in the Church claimed women should feel. I had come from a tradition where young girls had fought the Nazis and Soviet forces with all their might, running before continual fire as messengers, fighting as soldiers, being tortured, not giving in and dying if need be. Women could be resistance fighters, carry guns and do what needed to be done in Poland, Ireland or wherever. The nuns had given an example of constancy and strength. We had a rich education. I never had anything but respect for the Irish nuns who had come to transform Australia and considered them brave, ready to deal with overwhelming circumstances. Nor did I have any sense that I had to liberate myself and dance in the sanctuary yelling out that I have been oppressed by the patriarchy. It was rather the authoritarian ideologues I learned to avoid.

The greatest authentic liberation, in retrospect, was the quality of our education, which opened the doors to a deeply Western Catholic heritage. It also provided a unique stability in the post-war years for families which had to cope with the long term social, psychological and other effects of displacement. When we became Catholics we entered a family that had long been the greatest giver

In the new millennium with Esther Yee, former 1960s boarder at Brigidine, outside the shop from which I used to buy cakes for her. No doubt the owners have changed but a cake shop is in the same place! Esther became a pharmacist and we met up in later life.

Here I am on a visit back to the school in 2007.

The old and the new, at an ex-students' reunion in 2016. I am up the back and Frances Ridley is to the left. More contemporary students in uniform graciously served us. We were given a boxed lunch! It was in this room we sang, as 13-year-olds, songs with refrains such as 'Ri fol ri fol tole de ri riddle i do'.

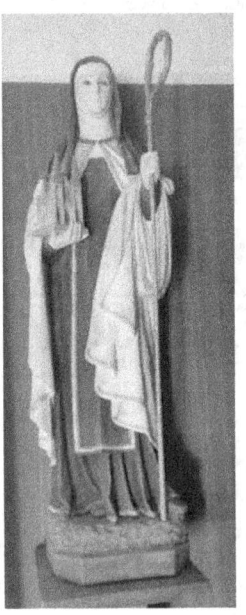

The statue of St Brigid of Kildare at Brigidine College is a constant reminder of the saint who inspired a teaching order of nuns.

of welfare in the world. Those organisations had worked well. Some may have needed reform, but did not deserve to disappear. The post-war generation, whoever they were, benefited immensely from the richness, sense of mission and Christ-like compassion of the parochial school system as it was then.

Final thoughts, mystery and silence

Saint John Paul II, in reflecting on the Second Vatican Council in 1995 when he was Pope, saw that the renewal of the Church (not a revolution) needed 'to begin with her mystery' thus drawing a contrast between earthly changes and spiritual ones.[48] Without doubt, that sense of mystery was conveyed to us. In the 1950s and 60s, reason, mystery, true silence, reflection and good foundational catechesis were pervasive, were 'normal' and fundamental to our spiritual formation in Catholic schools of the era, a basis for interior development. How could I not be grateful?

The fact of the Mass being in the vernacular was not, in my view, the cause of later problems in the Church as some suggest. It was rather the attitudinal, psychological change in that era: a politically manipulated retreat from reverence; a break in the spiritual *communio*. That can happen in any language if the right social forces prevail. For when I attended Latvian and Polish Masses in the vernacular in the 1960s and later, the sense of mystery still prevailed, so it was nothing to do with the language *per se*. The East European sensibility and consciousness of persecution could not but produce reflective silence. There was too much of a general sense of the supernatural and the apocalyptic dimensions of the Communist tragedy of recent times even to allow for a hint of jollity.

A cultural war had started during the latter part of the 1960s, of which most were unaware, and which would intensify in the 1970s, 80s and beyond. Terms such as 'liberation theology', 'Critical Theory' or 'cultural Marxism' were used to describe dimensions of that assault on parts of Western society. The effects of this onslaught were very powerful and, in my view, are yet to be fully understood in their historical and psychological dimensions. There is room for a species of 'psychologically focused history' to unravel the various threads of what was going on around us. In any case, even if we had understood it all, how could we have translated the notion of a growing cultural/spiritual war to happy, trusting believers? Most believed everything was fine, saw no danger in the cult of progress while the psychological weapons being used were invisible. Australia was the best country in the world, a haven for refugees, a land of 'blue horizons' and 'jewel seas'. Surely no invisible cultural guerrilla war could touch her?

It did touch her. Perhaps the most evocative image of the era to come, which left so many psychologically and spiritually wounded, is that of 'the field hospital', as Pope Francis put it. Many did become victims of the ideological assault on Christianity, the political correctness, beguiling media mantras or simply sheer confusion.

Going out the door

As we stood on the sunny threshold of a new world in 1969, however, enough of the Catholic vision had seeped through to give us the hope we could face anything. We were inheritors of a view of the cosmos over 2,000 years old. Stepping out, I had the legacies of Mother Pascal and all the other teachers who had transmitted an understanding of time and eternity. We headed out to pursue various paths in life, whether as teachers, doctors, nurses, academics, psychologists or musicians. Many married and became mothers, and one, Maree Marsh, became a Brigidine Sister. Perhaps the most unusual career was that of my childhood friend Karel, who after doing well at university, went on to become a black belt in martial arts and could throw people over her shoulder – 'only if I had to' she said – and instructed others to do likewise.

Perhaps some will disagree with my version of events and write their stories. May it be so. The more the better! But such is my vision embedded in unending gratitude to the nuns, priests and brothers who gave us so much – as intrepid teachers, generous missionaries, witnesses and thinkers.

As we joked and signed autograph books on our very last day at school, we wished each other well, all the while taking our spiritual heritage for granted. This Brigidine education, as an example of many Catholic schools of that time, with all its Irish idiom, eccentric moments and theological assurance, truly connected me to Chartres, Rome, the saints, every angel in the universe, its philosophers, writers, musicians and deep thinkers.

Without the spiritual resilience transmitted by the Brigidines and all the other nuns, brothers and priests who taught in that era, to whom this story pays great tribute, many of us would not have survived the looming deconstruction. The vortex of cultural revolution had taken hold, had power, but the transcendent realities, magnificent sense of history, expansive horizons and a distrust of worldly allures had their power too, and had taken root just in time. They gave us, even useless articles like me, so many pearls beyond price, such unforgettable, ineffable visions of immortality.

In the Sydney Brigidine College courtyard with the folly behind autumn leaves.

ENDNOTES

1 Mark Massa has written a comprehensive book on this post-war era in Catholic history and while it focuses on American experience, there are many similarities to the Australian Catholic culture of the time. Mark Massa. *Catholics and American Culture* (NY: Crossroad, 1999).

2 Edmund Campion, *Rockchoppers: Growing up Catholic in Australia* (Melbourne: Penguin Books, 1982), 48.

3 Summarised here from the *Catholic Encyclopedia* on the following website: https://www.catholicity.com/encyclopedia/p/polding,john_bede.html: 'Bishop Polding reached Sydney in September, 1835, and at once set to work to organize his vast diocese. He found only three priests in New South Wales and one in Tasmania; these with the three or four Benedictine monks whom he had brought with him constituted the entire force at his disposal. Then, and for many years afterwards, he worked like one of his priests, saying Mass daily in various stations, often in the convict prisons, teaching the Catechism, hearing the confessions of multitudes, and attending the sick and dying. He obtained permission to give retreats in the prison establishments, and between 1836 and 1841 no less than 7,000 convicts made at least ten days' retreat under his guidance. The authorities soon realized the good effect his influence was having, and arranged that, on the arrival of every ship-load of convicts, all the Catholics should be placed at his disposal for some days, during which the bishop and his assistants saw each prisoner personally and did all they could for them before they were drafted off to their various destinations.'

4 Janice Garaty, *Providence Provides* (Sydney: UNSW Press Book, 2013), 3. A comprehensive account of the Brigidine order of nuns in Australia.

5 Quoted in Garaty, op. cit., 4.

6 *Sydney Morning Herald*, 19 April 1953. http://trove.nla.gov.au/newspaper/article/18514055; there is another account as a pdf on the site: www.sydneycatholic.org/news/eucharist06/pdf/1953%20Procession.pdf.

7 *Sydney Morning Herald*, 16 April 1953. http://trove.nla.gov.au/newspaper/article/18368168.

8 Marrickville Heritage Society.

http://marrickville-heritage.blogspot.com.au/2012/10/marrickville-suburb-history.html (Accessed 12/4/2016)

9 Taken from St Nicholas Parish website: http://www.stnicholas.com.au/general/aboutourparishhistory

10 Ibid.

11 Carl Rogers, *On Becoming a Person: A Therapist's View of Psychotherapy* (Boston: Houghton Mifflin Co, 1961), particularly 90ff.

12 Ibid., 91, 104.

13 Vitz, *Psychology as Religion: The Cult of Self-Worship* (Grand Rapids: Eerdmans Publishing Company, 1977), 79-80; Vitz, 'Values Clarification in the Schools,' *New Oxford Review*, 48, June (1981), 16.

14 Edmund Campion, *A Place in the City* (Sydney: Penguin, 1994), 118.

15 St Brigid's Marrickville. Accessed from: http://stbrigid.org.au/about-us/our-history/

16 Ibid.

17 Ibid.

18 Ibid.

19 All quotations taken from the parish website history. http://www.stbrigidscoogee.org.au/our-parish/history

20 Campion, op. cit., 118.

21 Paul Connerton, *How Societies Remember* (UK, Cambridge University Press, 1989), 102-103.

22 Again Mark Massa gives a good account of this from the American point of view in: Mark Massa. *Catholics and American Culture* (NY: Crossroad, 1999).

23 Father Ranieri Cantalamessa, Special Advent Sermon 'The Universal Call to Holiness', 11 December 2015. http://insidethevatican.com/popeswords/specialevent/special-advent-sermon-by-fr-raniero-cantalamessa

24 J.P, Marmion. 'The Penny Catechism: A Long Lasting Text'. http://faculty.education.illinois.edu/westbury/paradigm/Marmion3.html

25 The entire *Penny Catechism* can be found online at: http://www.proecclesia.com/penny%20catechism/index.htm

26 Frances Phillips, 'Rediscovering the Stark Power of the Penny Catechism',

http://www.catholicherald.co.uk/commentandblogs/2015/02/17/rediscovering-the-stark-power-of-the-penny-catechism/

27 Most of the historical background information is taken from the website entitled: St Brigid's Coogee. http://www.stbrigidscoogee.org.au/our-parish/history

28 Ibid.

29 Details in these paragraphs are also taken from the following website: https://sites.google.com/a/syd.catholic.edu.au/stbcoogee/about-us/our-school

30 Gerard Henderson, *Bob Santamaria: a Most Unusual Man* (Melbourne, MUP, 2015); Greg Sheridan, *When We Were Young and Foolish* (Aus: Allen &Unwin, 2015).

31 Edmund Campion, *A Place in the City*, 108-9.

32 I was able to peruse these 'old' Annuals from the 1960s due to the kindness of the Brigidine Archivist, Sr Kathleen Butler.

33 It is very difficult to find a recording of this song online. Here is a link to students singing it: https://www.youtube.com/watch?v=boF2Na_z4Z0 (Accessed 23/11/2017).

34 James Franklin, *Catholic Values and Australian Realities* (Melbourne: Connor Court, 2006), 30ff.

35 James Franklin, *Corrupting the Youth: a History of Philosophy in Australia* (Sydney: Macleay Press, 2003).

36 Franklin, *Catholic Values and Australian Realities,* 40.

37 Tracey Rowland, 'The Authority of "Experts" and the Ethos of Modern Institutions,' *Communio: International Catholic Review*, Winter (2001), 746.

38 Kenneth L. Woodward, 'Reflections on the Revolution in Rome: Reporting the Catholic sixties', *First Things,* February (2013). https://www.firstthings.com/article/2013/02/reflections-on-the-revolution-in-rome?utm_source=First+Things+Subscribers&utm_campaign=db002fd4cb-

39 Aidan Nichols, OP, *The Council in Question: A Dialogue with Catholic Traditionalism* (UK, Gracewing, 2011), 52

40 One of his many good analyses is: Paul Kengor, *Takedown: From Communists to Progressives, How the Left Has Sabotaged Family and Marriage,* (USA, WND Books, 2015).

41 From the evidence of Soviet defectors. See, for example, the book *Disinformation* (2013) by Ion Mihai Pacepa and Ronald J. Rychlak. Pacepa, a Romanian, was the highest ranking KGB official ever to defect to the West (in 1978), and outlined the various methods of disinformation used on naive youth in Western countries.

42 An interesting short account of this topic can be found in: 'Cultural Marxism, Critical Theory, & The Frankfurt School' at: https://battlefieldamerica.wordpress.com/2012/01/19/cultural-marxism-critical-theory-the-frankfurt-school/

43 Tracey Rowland, *Culture and the Thomist Tradition* (London: Routledge, 2003), 35.

44 Michal Ion Pacepa's book *Disinformation* (2013) is a fascinating firsthand account of this.

45 Quoted in Paul Senz, 'Journalist Peter Seewald: Pope Benedict is "one of the most misunderstood personalities of our time"', *Catholic World Report*, 12/1/2017: http://www.catholicworldreport.com/Item/5342/journalist_peter_seewald_pope_benedict_is_one_of_the_most_misunderstood_personalities_of_our_time.aspx

46 This is discussed in Coulson, "The Story of a Repentant Psychologist," The Latin Mass, Vol. 3: 1 January-February (1994). http://www.ewtn.com/library/PRIESTS/COULSON.TXT (Accessed 14/9/08).

47 David Schindler discusses this in his work: *At the Heart of the World, from the Center of the Church* (Michigan: Eerdmans, 1996).

48 Saint John Paul II, '*Lumen Gentium* is Key to Council', Angelus Message, *L'Osservatore Romano*. Weekly Edition in English, 22 October 1995, 1,11.

www.ingramcontent.com/pod-product-compliance
Lightning Source LLC
Chambersburg PA
CBHW060951230426
43665CB00015B/2157